The Tragic Life

**Bessie Head
and
Literature in Southern Africa**

The Tragic Life

Bessie Head
and
Literature in Southern Africa

Edited by Cecil Abrahams

Africa World Press, Inc.

P.O. Box 1892
Trenton, New Jersey 08607

Africa World Press, Inc.
P. O. Box 1892
Trenton, NJ 08607

© Africa World Press, Inc., 1990

Cover design by Ife Nii Owoo

Library of Congress
Catalog Card Number: 90-81309

ISBN: 0-86543-176-0   Cloth
        0-86543-177-9   Paper

CONTENTS

Introduction

When Bessie Head died suddenly in Botswana in April 1986, she had already established for herself a major place as a writer in African literature. Her novels, especially *When Rain Clouds Gather* and *A Question of Power*, have been acclaimed as phenomenal achievements in the still youthful field of African writing. Her interest and dedication to her adopted land Botswana have through her study of the royal Khama clan brought the history and civilization of the Botswana people closer to the general public. Bessie Head expressed her psychological, social and political views with great vigour—whether she did this through her fictional or nonfictional work.

This collection of essays contains a variety of views from a number of scholars who have been fascinated by Bessie Head's literary mind. The first essay in the collection gives us an insight into a tortured existence which the writer herself used to great advantage in forming her literary output. Cecil Abrahams argues in "The Tragic Life of Bessie Head" that it is because of her early insecure beginnings that she continues to deal almost exclusively with the themes of madness, male brutality and the unfortunate racial problems which exist in southern Africa. In her own essay, "Social and Political Pressures that Shape Literature in Southern Africa", Bessie Head argues that the history of southern Africa is full of horrible details of crime by the state and by ordinary citizens against other citizens. This being so, it is easy, therefore, to understand why the literature of this region is dominated by horror and severe physical and mental brutalization of ordinary people.

In Carol Davison and Roger Berger's essays, there is an in-depth examination of the themes of personal and political madness that play such an important role in Bessie Head's work. Nancy Topping Bazin also looks at this phenomenon, but she tries to understand Head by comparing her consciousness with that of the Nigerian writer Buchi Emecheta.

We learn from Ella Robinson and Virginia Ola that the world Bessie Head lived in abounded with good and evil. Both of them go on to show how the writer dealt with these overwhelming presences. Through very close readings of Bessie Head's *Collector of Treasures*, Femi Ojo-Ade and Nigel Thomas describe the village people who made up the writer's work. Ezenwa-Ohaeto discusses the family in the short stories. Daniel Gover and Horace Goddard look at the imagery which unifies *Maru* and *A Question of Power*.

The twelve essays collected in this book should provide Bessie Head's students and friends with much to digest. It is hoped that these essays will suggest insights that can be explored in further detail. The further hope is that through this book Bessie Head will continue to remain an important and vibrant presence in the continuing development of African literature.

Cecil Abrahams
Brock University

The Tragic Life of Bessie Head

Cecil A. Abrahams

Bessie Head's auspicious birth and difficult physical and psychological development, in a country already beriddled by vicious racism, contributed greatly to her tragic existence both in South Africa and Botswana. The fact that she was racially a member of the Cape coloured community of South Africa, and yet never felt a part of this community, led her to a restless search for an identity within the confusing racial spectrum of southern Africa; and this insecurity contributed as well to her perception regarding the efficacy of organized political action.

Bessie Head's maternal grandparents came from England and her paternal ones were from South Africa. Since her birth was unordinary, she made no contact with either set of grandparents. Her mother, who was white, was admitted by her family to an asylum when she was discovered to be pregnant by their black stable boy. It was in this asylum where Head was born and where her mother committed suicide when Head was barely one year old. In what I consider to be her most successful and mature novel, *A Question of Power* (17), Head depicts the peculiarity of her position:

> First they received you from the mental hospital and sent you to a nursing-home. A day later you were returned because you did not look white. They sent you to a Boer family. A week later you were returned. The woman on the committee said: "what can we do with this child? Its mother is white".

Rejected in her formative years by the white community, her brown colour naturally made her a member of the Cape coloured community. It was, therefore, to a poor coloured family that she was sent to be brought up. She never felt at home in her adopted family and did not learn to become a full-fledged member of the coloured community. Indeed, she felt alienated not only inside South Africa, but in the coloured community. After completing her teacher's certificate and being involved for a short time as a teacher, she began to move restlessly around the country in search of peace and a secure home. She told me in an interview that she accepted the job of reporter to a weekly newspaper because it permitted her unsettled mind to rove around the country with the faint hope of finding a place to rest and to be at home inside herself. She thought that she would find such a niche in the coloured heart land of the Cape, but as he described it to me:

> Here were people with various shades of brown. Those who looked white, those who looked brown, and those who looked like Indians, and those who looked like Africans. As a newcomer to the Cape, I though I had found the ideal place for my mixed-race soul. But I quickly and painfully learned that if you were not fully grounded in the colour brown, you would have to be excluded from the community's business and be ready to endure insult. I knew then that I would not find rest in the God-forsaken country.
> *(Unpublished interview with C. Abrahams)*

Unlike most thinking South Africans who went into exile, Bessie Head left her homeland not only because she detested apartheid, but chiefly because she hoped to find peace in another country far from the racial sickness of South Africa. It is, therefore, not surprising, that her first novel set in Botswana, *When Rain Clouds Gather*, published in 1968, should emphasize so heavily the twin aspects of hope and despair. In subsequent works she continues to be preoccupied with the familiar South African themes of political and spiritual exile, racial hatred and the source of corrupting power and authority.

Bessie Head's fiction is in so many ways an attempt by her to come to some resolution of her mind with the questions of her racial identity and the particular burden that must be carried by those who are not a natural part of the indigenous society. The heroine of *A Question of Power*, which was published in 1974, is the coloured South African Elizabeth. She is regarded by the blacks of Botswana as a queer specimen of humanity who does not belong to either the white or black race. Furthermore, as in the case of Head, Elizabeth was born in a mental institution the daughter of an illegitimate and illegal relationship between a white woman and a black stable boy. Hence, Elizabeth makes her way through life with the twin-stigmas of being coloured and being predisposed towards madness. These are the haunting pressences in *A Question of Power*. It is Dan, the surface-reality, conventional, evil Medusa figure of the novel who constantly flouts these two areas of seeming weaknesses into Elizabeth's face and which often causes her to doubt her ability to logically examine and thus to overcome the difficulties which are suggested. Medusa or Dan suggests to Elizabeth that the Coloured people are not Africans, that they do not carry the ignoble pass book with all its insults and indignity, and that Coloureds do not speak an African language. Coloureds are "Dog, filth, [and the] Africans will eat [them] to death". Medusa wants her to accept her coloured race classification and the nightmare dream of Coloured men as "homosexuals" who parade "down the street in women's clothes" wearing "tied turbans round their heads" with "lipstick," fluttering "their eyes and hands" and talking "in high, falsetto voices". Medusa haunts Elizabeth at night with pictures of "all these coloured men ... on their backs, their penes in the air" and dying slowly. And Medusa reminds her: "you see, that's what you are like.... That's your people, not African people. You're too funny for words. You have to die like them." In the unexamined state of Medusa's accusation, Elizabeth retorts lamely and in terror that it was in fact to escape Medusa's cruel accusation that she left South Africa because she abhorred racism and sought its eradication. Thus the attack on her race and herself in Botswana by the blacks seems to her to be unjust and perverse. Instead of escaping once more the racial prejudice of man, Bessie Head seeks to examine the cause of the phenomenon of racism:

> There was nothing she could think of, to counter it: "I'm not like that. I've never been a racialist. Of course, I admit I'm a coloured. I'm not denying anything. Maybe people who are coloureds are quite nice too, just like Africans ...."

She had in fact escaped South Africa to be freed of the taint of racism which had been imposed on her by the whites. Hence she takes Elizabeth through the torturous, lonely journey of the soul knowing that the answers are not to be found in pious ritual or wisdom passed down by the sages, but "the real battlefront was living people, their personalities, their treatment of each other".

In *When Rain Clouds Gather*, Makhaya, the chief protagonist and exile from South Africa, finds it difficult at first to accept the genuine concern for goodness that is expressed by the Englishman Gilbert Balfour. Makhaya's natural instinct is to "distrust and dislike ... white people" because

> He had seen [white inhumanity] in the slums of all the cities of South Africa where black men had to live and how a man walked out of his home to buy a packet of cigarettes and never returned and how his seemingly senseless murder gave a brief feeling of manhood to a man who had none.

Makhaya searches for an answer to his dilemma, but his inconclusive response continues to leave him bitter. Life continues to be an "illusion of freedom" even though he has now found a meaningful occupation and a faithful and loving wife in Paulina Sebeso. He still sees himself as "the Black Dog" who is torturously tossed around by life.

In *Maru*, Bessie Head's second novel, which was published in 1971, the writer looks at racial prejudice as practised against the ancient Masarwa or Bushmen people. Again Head concerns herself with the outsider, in this case Margaret, the Masarwa girl who experiences prejudice at the hands of the narrow-minded Botswana society. In emphasing racial prejudice by one black group against another, Head demonstrates that racism is not peculiar to whites only. She illustrates that because of their particular racial colour and physical features, the Masarwa, though a black race, are regarded as the "low man" on the totem pole and must suffer all the injustices of that decreed position. Not only are the Masarwa referred to as "Bushman! Low Breed! Bastard!," they are spat upon and abused physically. Head concludes, therefore, that racism has a deep, psychic depth which goes beyond the more noticeable, visible occurrences of hatefulness:

> Before the white man became universally disliked for his mental outlook, it was there. The white man found only too many people who looked different. That was all that outraged the receivers of his discrimination, that he applied the technique of the wild jiggling dance and the rattling tin cans to anyone who was not a white man. And if the white man thought that Asians were a low, filthy nation, Asians could still smile with relief—at least, they

were not Africans [blacks]. And if the white man thought Africans were a low, filthy nation, Africans in Southern Africa could still smile—at least, they were not Bushmen. They all have their monsters. You just have to look different from them, ... then seemingly anything can be said and done to you as your outer appearance reduces you to the status of a non-human being.

In an Africa with hundreds of tribes who for centuries have warred against each other for minor reasons, this statement is very important. Indeed, the statement applies universally.

Much of the rest of *Maru* treats the daily occurrences of racial discrimination against the Masarwa girl, Margaret, and the lowly Masarwa servants who are regarded as slaves. Head's novel, unfortunately, has a fairy tale ending where Margaret mysteriously attracts Maru and this leads to a proposal of marriage. But the marriage does not change the prejudice and narrowness of the Botswana, they simply close their doors on their chief and withdraw their allegiance. But for the Masarwa, however, "a door silently opened on the small, dark airless room in which their souls had been shut for a long time". Then, almost out of character with the slow pace of the novel, Head defiantly proclaims:

> People like the Botswana, who did not know that the wind of freedom had also reached people of the Masarwa tribe, were in for an unpleasant surprise because it would be no longer possible possible to treat Masarwa people in an inhuman way without getting killed yourself.

The context of Bessie Head's final statement in *Maru* is the world of frustration and bitterness which both Makhaya and herself have experienced. They had both imagined that by escaping to Botswana they would "forget [South Africa] or throw it off", but both recognize that the past cannot be escaped, that the tyranny of the place South Africa will haunt them and turn their Botswana exile into "an illusion of freedom". Head concludes, therefore, that from her exiled position she must carefully examine the question of racism in South Africa, and, furthermore, she must propose her own solution.

Bessie Head differs with other South African writers, such as Alex La Guma, regarding the solution to the problem of racism and the inhumanity of one group towards another. In this instance, as well, her early life experiences contribute greatly towards her perception of the reality in South Africa. Although it is the apartheid and class systems which created terrible pain and separation for her parents, and which forced upon her a life of insecurity and hurt, she tends to react to that personal injury which she so often had to suffer at the hands of the more powerful in society. Hence, unlike La Guma, she seeks solutions in the nitty-gritty of face to face action and in the dark recesses of the human soul. As we have seen, in *When Rain Clouds Gather* and *Maru* she puts the blame of racist action on the shoulders of all mankind, not the whites only. In so doing, her novels are progressive in their philosophical conclusion on the nature and source of evil. Not being schooled in any political party or group ideology, she eschews "the lofty statements of mankind's great teachers". For her, Hell is to be overcome by exploring the inner personal hells that every person must experience and not by "indistinct statements about evil". Hence, she teaches characters such as Makhaya and Elizabeth that "It was harder to disclose the subtle balances of power between people" and that "people with soft shuffling, loosely-knit personalities [were] preyed upon by dominant, powerful persons".

Head's journey into the darkness of the human soul, that evil which visited her before her birth and drove her into haunting exile, takes her to three sources of evil and, hence, goodness. The most obvious source for the political exile is the world of power and authority: the belief that if the political institutions which decree and regulate the lives of the society are reformed or abolished a better or new society can be established. But as Makhaya and Elizabeth discover that even in a black-dominated political structure, their lives are not secure. Chief Matenge informs Makhaya that "You know what a South African swine is? He is a man like you. He always needs to run after his master, the white man." Here, as in the case of Dan or Medusa in *A Question of Power*, it is the power of the elite, be it white or black, which creates prejudice against them. Head concludes, then, that if political institutions which make the monstrous decisions were to be transformed for the good, then the source of their evil is to be found more fundamentally in their hierarchical power structure.

Bessie Head's fiction leads back, again and again, to the corrupt, greedy and power hungry elite of politicians, tribal chiefs and teachers. She singles out the African politician in *When Rain Clouds Gather* because Makhaya had in South Africa regarded the African politician as the saviour of the oppressed. It is Makhaya who learns that the politicians are generally like Joas Tsepe. During colonial rule these politicians declare themselves as the true revolutionaries who will liberate the oppressed. When colonial rule ends and through democratic means these politicians are not elected to govern, they join the reactionary establishment of the society and declare war on the government. The reactionary establishment is the continuing tribal system of local government by the chiefs. Generally, the chiefs, who were rich and powerful men in the colonial system, because of their diminishing intake of wealth and authority align themselves with the disgruntled politicians. The chiefs, then, become a hindrance to development on both a spiritual and physical level, and they continue to encourage race prejudice, narrowness, myopic tribalism and corruption.

It is in *A Question of Power* that Head finds an answer to her search for man's evil and his good. And it is here that she realizes that the political and economic institutions can truly be transformed for the betterment of man when man has analyzed and resolved the questions of good and evil embedded in his soul. Hence, Botswana, the place of escape, becomes the area where there is a "total de-mystifying of all illusions". In thinking that they have escaped the "filth" of South Africa, Makhaya and Elizabeth are challenged even more intensely to understand the causes for the South African "filth" and to transform it from deadness into a living hope. This is the "beautiful world of the future" that Sello prophesies for Elizabeth's future. The world of the future must be freed of the Medusa power seekers and elite authority. And to accomplish this task Elizabeth and Makhaya must dedicate themselves to eradicating evil in all its forms. By doing so, they will discover the true meaning of "Gods." The "Gods," says Sello, are those ordinary people who have dedicated their lives to fighting evil:

> It seemed to her as though all suffering gave people and nations a powerful voice fur the future and a common meeting-ground, because the types of people Sello referred to as "the Gods" turned out on observation to be ordinary, practical, sane people, seemingly their only distinction being that they had consciously concentrated on spiritual earnings. All the push and direction was towards the equality of man in his soul, as though, if he were not fixed up there, it never would be anywhere else ....

Bessie Head's approach to the South African problem is, then, from within the soul of man. It is pointless, says Sello, to hate the racist whites for what oppression they have and continue to inflict on the black people of South Africa. As racists, they are not free, they simply imprison their souls in their own cobweb of hatred. Their racism must be overcome through love and not violence, nor through the deceptive power-seeking black elite of Africa. Bessie Head, therefore, opposed vehemently organized class action and sought solutions on the personal level. Although she differed in this way with most other South African writers, I believe that her solution is as valid in the South African reality as that of the other writers. However, personal solutions demand greater endurance and thus often greater hope and despair. That these solutions were not possible in her own lifetime merely added to the tragedy of Bessie Head's painful existence.

Social and Political Pressures that Shape Literature in Southern Africa

Bessie Head

In some inexplicable way the South American writer, Gabriel Garcia Marquez, captured the whole soul of ancient Southern African history in a few casual throw-away lines in his novel *One Hundred Years of Solitude*: (p. 20)

> ... In the small separate room, where the walls were gradually being covered by strange maps and fabulous drawings, he taught them to read and write and do sums, and he spoke to them about the wonders of the world, not only where his learning had extended, but forcing the limits of his imagination to extremes. It was in that way that the boys ended up learning that in the southern extremes of Africa there were men so intelligent and peaceful that their only pastime was to sit and think ....

This astonishing observation on life in Southern Africa occurs at the very beginning of the novel and except that insofar as it is indicative of the author's vast range of intellectual compassion, the quote I use is quite unrelated to the general development of the novel's themes and preoccupations. What is so astonishing is the accuracy of the observation. Southern African history is associated with so many horrors—police states, detentions, sudden and violent mass protests and death, exploitation and degrading political systems. Any thought that it could have once been one of "the wonders of the world" seems unreal.

And yet, long ago, before the period of colonial invasion, it was a beautiful world. The British historian, Anthony Sillery, in his book *Founding a Protectorate* (p. 70), gives a little indication of life in Southern Africa before it was almost totally conquered by foreign powers:

> ... at the beginning of the Scramble for Africa the
> southern route presented to Great Britain the most
> readily available means of access to the interior ...
> Southern Africa, especially for an Englishman,
> was a friendly country. The chiefs, many of them
> courteous, civilized men, were hospitable, and the
> people helpful and only rarely aggressive .....

Sillery contrasts this with the difficulties the invaders faced in their attempts to conquer East and North Western Africa. The tribes were generally "rapacious, suspicious, extortionate and warlike and the interior filled with steamy, fetid swamps through which nothing but a canoe could travel."

I was born in South Africa and that is synonymous with saying that one is born into a very brutal world—if one is black. Everything had been worked out by my time and the social and political life of the country was becoming harsher and harsher. A sense of history was totally absent in me and it was as if, far back in history, thieves had stolen the land and were so anxious to cover up all traces of the theft that correspondingly, all traces of the true history have been obliterated. We, as black people, could make no appraisal of our own worth; we did not know who or what we were, apart from objects of abuse and exploitation. Each nation offers the world a little of its light; each nation boasts of the great men who shaped its destiny. We had a land that offered the world only gold; no great men were needed to articulate the longings of the people. In a creative sense I found myself left only with questions. How do we and our future generations resolve our destiny? How do we write about a world long since lost, a world that never seemed meant for humans in the first place, a world that reflected only misery and hate? It was my attempt to answer some of these questions that created many strange divergences in my own work.

Botswana is so close to South Africa that barely a night's journey by train separates the two countries from each other. Botswana was the former British Bechuanaland Protectorate which became independent in 1966. In my eyes Botswana is the most unique and distinguished country in the whole of Africa. It has a past history that is unequalled anywhere in Africa. It is a land that was never conquered or dominated by foreign powers and so a bit of ancient Africa, in all its quiet and unassertive grandeur, has remained intact there. It became my home in 1964.

When I was first published in 1968, a London literary agent

wrote to me as follows: "... There isn't much of a market for South African literature here in England. People don't seem to be so interested in it. But you have new experiences by having lived in Botswana. Let us see what you can make of it ...."

I cannot pretend to be a student of South African literature; I cannot assess its evolution or lack of evolution. I only feel sure that the main function of a writer is to make life magical and to communicate a sense of wonder. I do admit that I found the South African situation so evil that it was impossible for me to deal with, in creative terms. A British visitor to South Africa once said to me: "You arrive in South Africa and see all those black faces. And you think: 'They must have the same sensitivities and feelings as we do.' But no matter how much you think this the system beams at you that all those black faces are not human and you leave the country without having any communication with black people at all ...."

It was this nightmare sense of despair that was suddenly lifted from me. Literature is very functional in Southern Africa and bound inextricably to human suffering; the death of South African literature is that it is almost blinded by pain; people hardly exist beside the pain. I found myself performing a peculiar shuttling movement between two lands. All my work had Botswana settings but the range and reach of my preoccupations became very wide. People, black people, white people, loomed large on my horizon. I began to answer some of the questions aroused by my South African experience.

My work has covered the whole spectrum of Southern African preoccupations—refugeeism, racialism, patterns of evil, and the ancient Southern African historical dialogue.

Refugeeism. Refugees flood into Botswana from three points— South-West Africa (Namibia), Rhodesia (Zimbabwe), and South Africa. In 1967 I was officially registered as a South African refugee and for two years I lived with the refugee community in Northern Botswana. My first novel, *When Rain Clouds Gather,* grew out of this experience. It was a fearfully demoralising way of life, of unemployment and hand-outs from the World Council of Churches. Liberation and power loomed large on the horizon for refugees from Zimbabwe and due to this they were the only refugees at that time who were regularly air-lifted out of Botswana for military training. They were all in opposing camps and their quarrels about power were violent and brutal. A young refugee from Zimbabwe quietly detached himself from the group and held long dialogues with me. He wanted an alternative to war and power. He had no faith in the future black leadership of Zimbabwe. There was no one articulating the hopes of the people and he did not want to die for a worthless cause. I latched eagerly on to his dialogue and my first novel provides an alternative for young men. I created a symbolic type of refugee personality. I implied that he was a man of talent. I made him briefly face the implications of black power and then turned him abruptly away from the madding crowd to spend a lifetime in a small rural village, battling with food production problems.

My first novel is important to me in a personal way. It is my only truly South African work, reflecting a black South African viewpoint. The central character in the novel, a black South African refugee, is almost insipid, a guileless, simple-hearted simpleton. But that is a true reflection of the black South African personality. We are an oppressed people who have been stripped bare of every human right. We do not know what it is like to have our ambitions aroused, nor do we really see liberation on an immediate horizon. Botswana was a traumatic experience to me and I found the people, initially, extremely brutal and harsh, only in the sense that I had never encountered human ambition and greed before in a black form.

Racialism. With all my South African experience I longed to write an enduring novel on the hideousness of racial prejudice. But I also wanted the book to be so beautiful and so magical that I, as the writer, would long to read and re-read it. I achieved this ambition in an astonishing way in my second nove, *Maru.* In Botswana they have a conquered tribe, the Masarwa or Bushmen. It is argued that they were the true owners of the land in some distant past, that they had been conquered by the more powerful Botswana tribes and from then onwards assumed the traditional role of slaves. Masarwa people were also abhorrent to Botswana people because they hardly looked African, but Chinese. I knew the language of racial hatred but it was an evil exclusively practised by white people. I therefore listened in amazement as Botswana people talked of the Masarwa whom they oppressed:

> "They don't think," they said. "They don't know anything."
> For the first time I questioned blind prejudice: "How do they know that? How can they be sure that the Maswara are not thinking?"

The research I did among Botswana people for *Maru* gave me the greatest insights and advantages to work right at the roots of racial hatred. I found out above all that that type of exploitation and evil is dependent on a lack of communication between the oppressor and the peeople he oppresses. It would horrify an oppressor to know that his victim has the same longings, feelings, and sensitivities as he has. Nothing prevented a communication between me and Botswana people and nothing prevented me from slipping into the skin of a Masarwa person. And so my novel was built up in blinding flashes of insights into an evil that hung like the sickness of death over all black people in South Africa.

Patterns of Evil. My third novel, *A Question of Power*, had such an intensely personal and private dialogue that I can hardly place it in the context of the more social and outward-looking work I had done. It was a private philosophical journey to the sources of evil. I argued that people and nations do not realise the point at which they become evil; but once trapped in its net, evil has a powerful propelling motion into a terrible abyss of destruction. I argued that its form, design, and plan could be clearly outlined and that it was little understood as a force in the affairs of mankind.

The Ancient Southern African Historical Dialogue

If one wishes to reach back into ancient Africa, the quality of its life has been preserved almost intact in Botswana. It is a world that moves so slowly that it seems to be asleep within itself. It is like a broad, deep, unruffled river and as accommodating. Anything that falls into its depth is absorbed. No new idea stands sharply aloof from the social body, declaiming its superiority. It is absorbed and transformed until it emerges somewhere along the line as "our traditional custom." Everything is touched by "our traditional custom"—British Imperialism, English, Independence, new educational methods, progress, and foreigners. It all belongs. So deep is people's sense of security that their general expression is one of abstraction and quiet absent-mindedness.

Botswana is one of those countries that survive by sheer luck and unexpected good fortune. On several occasions it teetered on the brink of being absorbed into Rhodesia or being governed by South Africa. During the period of colonial occupation, it produced two of the greatest black leaders the continent may ever know—Khama, The Great, and his son, Tshekedi Khama—men distinguished for their personal integrity and the power with which they articulated the hopes of their people. During the period of colonial occupation the British scoured the land from end to end in an endeavour to uncover its mineral wealth. Accidentally, after independence, the largest diamond mine in the world was discovered by a jet plane photographing the Kalahari desert with an infrared light camera. It is thought that had the British still been in control they would have wrecked the country rather than forsake such wealth.

Botswana benefitted by the catastrophe which fell upon South Africa. At the time of exploration into the interior all black chiefs were illiterate. They were helplessly dependent on verbal explanations given to them about documents which appealed for gold and diamond exploration concession rights. The verbal explanations never tallied with the contents of the documents, which dealt with the wholesale purchase of the land by the foreign invaders. In African custom the land could never be bought or sold; it could be apportioned for use to foreigners who had been befriended by the tribe or who had rendered services. The above and many other fraudulent means, like intoxicating the chiefs with brandy and then getting them to sign concession documents, were used to wrest the land from the tribes. Most of the tribes of South Africa were landless by the 1830s when foreign invasion reached the southern tip of Botswana.

Then a reaction set in. The powerful London Missionary Society which had its headquarters at Kuruman, near the southern tip of Botswana, began to campaign about the land question. Missionaries like John Mackenzie wrote books and papers exposing the means by which the land had been taken from black people and the suffering which ensued. The land question and almost every other question relevant to the black man's destiny converged in Botswana. It is on record that the British did not want Botswana. In their despatches they called it "a God-awful country to live in." It was grim and unproductive, subject to seven-year cycles of severe drought. It was called the "thirstland" by the early explorers as surface water was almost non-existent. Eventually, the country was given a general blanket coverage of "British Protection" because its only advantage to the British was that the land was almost uniformly level and provided an ideal situation for a railway line through to the interior. Apart from the railway line, they left the land and the people intact and undisturbed. Botswana uniquely remained black man's country.

The people could still have been destroyed by so many hostile forces—the northward thrust of the Afrikaner Boer, the

Germans and the Portuguese. It was not the British who sought out Botswana but the people of Botswana who sought out the British. A vague feeling floated in the air at that time that it was only the British who could be trusted to have honest dealings with black people. Yes, where financial greed was not a major British concern, the British took time off to hold exquisite dialogues of integrity.

Corresponding to the time of the declaration of the British Protectorate, Botswana produced a leader of such magnificence, Khama III or Khama, the Great, that the British bowed in awe and deference before him. His standards of integrity were so high that the British conceded to him what they would not concede to any black man at that time—a voice in Britain during the scramble for Africa. Thus, the details of foreign occupation were meticulously worked out. Although the country attracted few white settlers due to the harshness of its climate, the few who came in entered on tiptoe and minded their p's and q's. Khama III established a tradition whereby the chiefs of the land maintained a control over government and trade and he also retained the right, during his rule, to deport any white settler or missionary who displeased him.

The people of the land were never exposed to or broken by the sheer stark horror of white domination. They kept on dreaming as from ancient times and they kept alive the portrait of ancient Africa. It was this peaceful world of black people simply dreaming in their own skins that I began to slowly absorb into my own life. It was like finding black power and black personality in a simple and natural way. If the country is destroyed in the post-independence years, it will be by horrors within itself and not by foreign powers.

Works Cited

Gabriel Garcia Marquez. *One Hundred Years of Solitude*. London: Penguin, 1972.
Anthony Sillery. *Founding a Protectorate: History of Bechuanaland*. London: Mouton & Co., 1965.

A Method in the Madness

Carol Margaret Davison

In his highly illuminating and original study entitled *Madness and Civilization* (1961), the eminent French psychologist and philosopher Michel Foucault describes mental illness as a phenomenon that has—from the fifteenth century onwards—both fascinated and haunted the Western male imagination. Ranging from Charlotte Perkins Gilman's *The Yellow Wallpaper* (1892) to Sylvia Plath's *The Bell Jar* (1963), women's fictional depictions of madness over the past century exhibit a similar haunting fascination. These feminist visions, however, bear a radical stamp that aligns them with recent controversial psychiatric studies examining the nature and function of mental illness classification. In these contemporary socio-clinical analyses, exhausted and double-edged psychiatric rhetoric surrounding mental disorder is dealt a revolutionary blow, crystallized in Doctor Thomas S. Szasz's question: "Is the aim of psychiatry the study of human behavior or the control of human (mis)behaviour?"—'(mis)behavior' in this instance referring to any action deemed 'deviant' and, thus, a threat to the existing power structure.

In light of Szasz's query, madness may be described as the most potentially subversive subject in women's fiction, for the reassessment of female insanity necessitates its corollary—the reappraisal of patriarchal sanity. The attraction to the subject is, therefore, apparent. Moreover, it is appropriate, for in giving voice to her silenced sister, the woman writer underlines her own tragic legacy of voicelessness—an inheritance better described as a disinheritance. To adapt a phrase from Ellison's *Invisible Man*, on the lower frequencies the asylum-bound female speaks for all women.[4]

The recently defined female *bildungsroman* is the most potentially subversive genre in women's fiction and is popularly and appropriately employed in novels depicting women's madness. As Ellen Morgan argues in her article, "Humanbecoming: Form and Focus in the Neo-Feminist Novel," this genre has become "the most salient form of literature" used by contemporary women authors writing about women.[5] It radically subverts the developmental movement of the established genre which "embodies the Goethean model of organic growth: cumulative, gradual [and] total"[6] for it considers this an unrealistic movement that dangerously whitewashes differences of gender, race and class. The notion of silencing again arises, for while white male protagonists "struggle to find a hospitable context in which to realize their aspirations, female protagonists must frequently struggle to voice any aspirations whatsoever."[7] Recognizing, therefore, that society does not constrain men and women, black and white, nor rich and poor equally, the female *bildungsroman* foregrounds "difference" and forces a re-examination of the socio-political context of the narrative.

Coupled with the subversive subject of madness, the female bildingsroman may be poetically described as a literary lethal weapon. Two women's novels in the last twenty-five years skillfully combine this subject and genre: Jean Rhys' *Wide Sargasso Sea* (1966) and Bessie Head's *A Question of Power* (1974). Although they end in dramatically different ways and are stylistically at odds, both stories furnish disturbing visions of women's madness within similar colonial/cultural contexts and successfully challenge traditionally accepted social classifications and narrative structures. There is a method in Antoinette Cosway's (Rhys' protagonist) and Elizabeth's (Head's protagonist) madness that allows them to retain and/or to regain a certain sanity. Confronted with the brutalizing effects of colonialism, both novels confirm the unrelenting hopefulness of the marginalized woman.

Clara Thomas's astute description of *Wide Sargasso Sea* as culturally determined "psycho-biography"[8] is equally applicable to *A Question of Power*. Antoinette and Elizabeth are simultaneously conditioned and victimized by their social and familial environments. Torn between two cultures, they exist metaphorically as women of the penumbra for whom marginalization is prescribed. As a white creole woman in the West Indies, Antoinette is regarded as "an outcast, a sort of freak rejected by both Europe and England, whose blood she shares, and by the black West Indian people, whose culture and home have been hers for two generations or more.[9] As a mulatto woman, Elizabeth is similarly regarded as a 'misfit' both in her native South Africa and in her newly adopted home of Motabeng, Botswana.

To add fuel to the fires of ostracism, both protagonists are plagued by what others consider to be a genetic predisposition to madness. The faulty gene is, significantly, traced back to their mothers in both cases. In South Africa's colour-coded society, Elizabeth's white mother defied the fundamental low of the Apartheid system (the Immorality Act of 1957) by "having a child by the stable boy, who was a native"[10] As a result, she was promptly locked away in the local mental hospital, and her daughter abandoned to deal with "the stigma of insanity" (17). As the malicious principal of Elizabeth's mission school warns her:

> 'We have a full docket on you. You must be careful. Your mother was insane. If you"re not careful you"ll get insane just like your mother'
> (16)

As a stranger in Jamaica, Antoinette's Martinican mother, Annette, is singled out as the scapegoat in her society. Ridiculed by her black and white neighbours, Annette only succumbs to breakdown following the deliberate burning of her home and the subsequent death of her favourite child, Pierre.[11] Like Elizabeth, Antoinette inherits the stigma of insanity—a myth that is reinforced in Part Two of *Wide Sargasso Sea* when Daniel Cosway cautions Antoinette's English husband, Edward Rochester: "There is madness in that family" for her father and grandfather both "die[d] raving" (180). For the mentally unstable Rochester, Antoinette's mother's madness substantiates the case.

Labelled and rejected in childhood, Antoinette and Elizabeth embark upon the critical and almost impossible quest for self-definition and self-actualization. Embroiled in what exiled South African writer Ezekiel Mphahlele calls "the tyranny of place",[12] they are not unlike Milton's Satan in *Paradise Lost* who can not escape hell because he is hell personified.[13] Translated into their circumstances, Antoinette and Elizabeth can not escape madness because they have been socially defined as madness embodied. Confronted on all sides with such an overwhelming sense of limitation, both women avoid social interaction and withdraw into themselves. Antoinette's childhood maxim that everything is "better than people" (24) is echoed in the isolated Elizabeth's statement to her doctor that she does not like people (51).

Oppressive forces continually assault both protagonists as they grow into adulthood. Elizabeth's troubled life in South Africa is compounded with her marriage to a perverse, molesting husband (18), and Antoinette's desperate and persistent quest for refuge from a brutal world also culminates in a hellish marriage that leads to her ultimate undoing. Antoinette's marriage to Rochester parallels her mother's marriage to Mr. Mason who, armed with his 'White Man's Burden' philosophy, "rescued ... [Antoinettee's family] from poverty and misery" (29) following the Emancipation Act of 1833. Antoinette's marriage, however, bears a warped twist. In the true fashion of plundering colonizer, Rochester methodically extracts wealth from the colony in the form of Antoinette's thirty thousand pound dowry (59), extinguishes her love of the unnamed Windward Island which represents her last remaining touchstone of safety and sanity (121), and forces her to relocate to England where he imprisons her in a dark, closeted room.

Anotinette's thwarted search for refuge is marked by a disastrous Sisyphean cyclical movement characteristic of the female *bildungsroman*. Spiritual development occurs, but it *can not* be transformed into action. Rochester's power over Antoinette lies primarily in his capacity with language, and although she gains an awareness of his cunning techniques, she remains powerless to alter her circumstances. Sold in the colonial marketplace, Antoinette is skillfully silenced by this one-man South Africa. Rochester reduces her to "silence itself" (138), "the queen of the silent night" (70) about whom he sings. Following their marriage, her voice is suffocated by Rochester's[14] as he labels his helpless wife a "lunatic" and "mad girl" (136, 140). Antoinette's voice, however, only reveals disturbance when it resurfaces in Part Three after she has relocated to England. Her breakdown is clearly prompted by this change of place—the crowning act of Rochester's hatred that, ironically, confirms that his purported "sanity" is actually "a form of socially sanctioned madness."[15]

In contrast, Antoinette's clarity of understanding is a testament to her retention of sanity despite her tragic situation. She grows to understand the fluid nature of experience and the precarious duplicity of the language that defines and communicates it. It is Antoinette who underlines the relativity of perception when she reminds her husband that there is always another side to every story (106).[16] She reiterates this point later in the novel when she questions Rochester's description of slavery as "a question of justice" (121). She remarks:

> 'Justice ... I've heard that word. It's a cold word. I tried it out ... I wrote it down. I wrote it down several times and always it looked like a damn cold lie to me. There is no justice.' (121)

These are sad but fitting words for Antoinette to employ, for she herself becomes a slave of sorts, locked away in Rochester's prison of Thornfield Hall. Knowledge of such injustice, however, does not serve to liberate her.

Although destructive acts, the burning down of Thornfield Hall and Antoinette's suicide are the only statements left to her within this dystopia. Suicide is, unfortunately, the most prevalent conclusion for women's novels of development,[17] but to designate self-destruction solely as a constructive action is to detract from Rhys's social critique. A universe wherein Rochester is classified as sane and Antoinette as insane is, indeed disturbing. This suicidal ending, however, remains paradoxically affirmative and negative. Moreover, it is in keeping with Antoinette's divided state throughout the entire novel. The burning of Thornfield Hall that closes *Wide Sargasso Sea* parallels the conflagration of Coulibri Estate during Antoinette's childhood (32-38), and connects her to the oppressed-but-conscious former West Indian slaves who rebelled against her family. Eternally trapped in limbo between two worlds, the creole Antoinette Cosway jumps from the battlements toward a vision of her ambivalent black childhood friend, Tia (155), who earlier rejected her (38)—a rather undevelopmental movement for a woman's novel of development.

Although Rhys and Head examine stigmatized women in similar circumstances, their final visions are separated by a wide sargasso sea. While Antoinette destroys both her prison and herself, Elizabeth rejects her deathlike state of madness and constructively reels toward life (203). She moves from introspection to activity—a movement rarely accomplished in the female *bildungsroman*. Elizabeth's act of piecing together the jigsaw wreckage of her emotional life is, however, a devastatingly painful and complicated process that extends over a three-year period (196). As in the Osiris-Isis myth that Head employs as a central metaphor (39, 40), Elizabeth (like the dismembered Osiris) successfully heals her fragmented self.

Precipitated by her relocation to Botswana from the schizophrenic South African Apartheid system, Elizabeth's descent into a "nightmare world of no compassion" (196) draws the reader into a terrifying maelstrom of madness and power politics. Unlike Antoinette's mind which acts—like the convent she enters—as a place of refuge from people and a tormented external world (24), Elizabeth's mind becomes the main arena for a power war between several "large, looming soul personalities (57) who have effectively persecuted her since her childhood in South Africa. Dan, the two

Sellos, and their various malicious accomplices (like Medusa) obscenely abuse Elizabeth's emotional/spiritual state, and confront her with internal war at a point when she finally expects peace. Having committed the sane act of fleeing from a brutal husband and an insane socio-political system, Elizabeth soon discovers that power politics are not exclusive to her homeland. In Botswana she reflects how:

> ... the evils overwhelming her were beginning to
> sound like South Africa from which she had fled.
> The reasoning, the viciousness were the same, but
> this time the faces were black ... (57)

This realization initially overwhelms the victimized Elizabeth who yearns for a sane refuge. The discovery, however, forces her toward greater social understanding and self-reliance.

As her hellish descent progresses, Elizabeth unweaves the complex web of the victim-victimizer relationship and comes to understand (like Antoinette) the victimizer's various methods for retaining control. She soon recognizes that the exclusive and savagely cruel system of witchcraft in Botswana (21) involves deceptive power politics that nullify the individual's free will to change her circumstances. Dan's exclusive prophecies play a similar role, for Elizabeth's belief in their inevitability renders her powerless to alter the course of her breakdown. Ultimately, she casts witchcraft and these prophecies aside, dismantles the God-man power dialectic that subjugates all people, and embraces a humanitarian perspective based on total equality. She decisively adheres to Sello-the-Monk's belief that "God is people. There's nothing up there. It's all down here" (109). Through this philosopy, Elizabeth begins to perceive that "madness is, indeed, man's derisive name for any speech (value system) that is not of his making, within his system of logic and acceptability and therefore under his control."[18] With this firmly in mind, Elizabeth recognizes that the patronizing Dane, Camilla, who never sees "black people as people but as objects of permanent idiocy" (76), is the actual "half-mad woman" (79).

Elizabeth's final state of complete integration synthesizes an internal and an external labour. Her successful vegetable garden is the external symbol of her creative act of regaining a foothold on life. Elizabeth's early act of renaming Motabeng—which traditionally means "the place of sand" (19)—"The Village of The Rain-Wind" (20) signals her fundamentally positive outlook. This mental act of renaming is transferred into physical action when Elizabeth—with the help of Kenosi, Tom, and Eugene—slowly builds up her garden in the local industries project. Through this external labour, she stakes her claim as an active inhabitant of Motabeng, and decisively throws off her marginalized status. Elizabeth's madness, therefore, acts as a metaphoric period of gestation out of which she emerges reborn—a movement that stands in stark contrast to Antoinette's slow reel towards death. Elizabeth's final act of placing "one soft hand over her land" and falling into peaceful sleep (206) signals both her triumph over an extended diabolical nightmare, and her capacity to endure the excruciating.[19]

Their ultimate visions may differ, but Jean Rhys and Bessie Head convey similar messages about male power and female powerlessness. Along the particular lines of gender politics, both novels examine the traditional problem of women's sexuality in the female *bildungsroman*.[20] In Elizabeth's and Antoinette's inverted worlds, healthy female sexuality is categorized as "deviant" and subsequently punished. The Medusa in *A Question of Power* who haunts Elizabeth's mind, flaunts her sexual prowess and attacks her victim by reducing her to sexlessness (44). Dan commits similar crimes against Elizabeth's sexuality with his "nice-time girls" (197) in Part Two. As the main goal of Elizabeth's odyssey is spritual, she rejects the sexual obsession of her nightmare *avatars*. She maintains that the vagina is "not such a pleasant area of the body to concentrate on, possibly only now and then if necessary" (44). In *Wide Sargasso Sea*, Rochester plays the role of asylum master[21] who defines Antoinette's natural sexuality as unnatural lust. Christophine's words explaining that Antoinette is "thirsty" for Rochester are misconstrued in his warped mind as he contemplates how Antoinette will:

> loosen her black hair, and laugh and coax and flatter (a mad girl. She'll not care who she's loving.) She'll moan and cry and give herself as no sane woman would—or could. *Or could*. (135-136)

These thoughts betray Rochester's façade of sexual normalcy. His unremorseless act of committing adultery with the malicious Amélie, while Antoinette lies in the adjoining room (115), again illustrates his perverse projection technique of blaming the victim. Rochester effectively employs obeah against Antoinette by renaming her 'Bertha' (121) and projecting all of his fears about himself onto this fictitious female. He proves, in the final analysis, to be the equivalent of "the master of the psychology behind witchcraft" (21) who terrorizes Elizabeth in *A Question of Power*. While Antoinette sadly succumbs to this death grip, Elizabeth survives it and forges her own self-definition.

Subversive in their structural and thematic concerns, *Wide Sargasso Sea* and *A Question of Power* diverge along aesthetic lines. Rhys's penetrating and poetic analysis of madness demonstrates her unquestionable power over language—a capacity in which she clearly outdoes Edward Rochester. Hers is a beautifully constructed novel, rich with vibrant, imagistic language and cleverly interwoven themes. While Elizabeth is employed as Head's mouthpiece to issue an attack on the complex roots of society's ills, Antoinette acts as a subtle yet unmistakeable indicator that something is rotten in the state of human relationships. Bessie Head's didactic approach tends, at times, to stifle her art and to detract from her message. Perhaps the primary reason for this weakness in *A Question of Power* derives from the fact that Head translated her own experience of mental breakdown into story form.[22] Her depiction is, however, hauntingly powerful, for the reader experiences the Dantean depths of infernal madness with Elizabeth. Head's clinical portrait stands counter to Rhys's which remains distanced from the actual experience of mental illness. In this, Rhys's depiction may be classified as metaphorical and symbolic. It is quite surprising, therefore, that Head's realistic portrait of insanity concludes more positively. For this "rather rare" movement in African fiction,[23] she must be highly commended. This conclusion may be, as Cecil Abrahams writes, "frustrating to the more militant oppressed, [but it] is new in its context."[24] Although Bessie Head may be faulted for aspects of her aesthetic style, it is she who provides a more uplifting feminist vision. While Rhys returns the reader to the cavernous depths of distorted human relationships, Head constructs desperately needed bridges, and points the way to the more positive female *bildungsroman* of the future.

Notes

1 Michel Foucault, *Madness and Civilization: A History of Insanity in the Age of Reason* (1965; New York: Vintage Books, 1973) 15, 23. For the purposes of this paper, the blanket terms "madness", "insanity", and "mental illness" are employed interchangeably throughout, and specifically refer—within the contexts of the two examined novels—to schizophrenia (ranging from "simple schizophrenia" to "paranoid schizophrenia"). For the clinical symptoms of these mental disorders, I have relied upon Chapter Thirteen ("Schizophrenic and Paranoid Disorders") in Ian Gregory and Donald J. Smeltzer's *Psychiatry: Essentials of Clinical Practice* (Boston: Little, Brown and Company, 1977) 175-190.

2 Approaching madness from the point of social control, see in particular all of Andrew Scull's books on madness; Thomas S. Szasz's *The Myth of Mental Illness: Foundations of a Theory of Personal Conduct* (1961; London: Granada Publishing Limited, 1972), and *Ideology and Insanity: Essays on the Psychiatric Dehumanization of Man* (Garden City: Doubleday & Company, Inc., 1970); Malcolm Lader's *Psychiatry on Trial* (Harmondswowrth: Penguin, 1977); and Elaine Showalter's fascinating study *The Female Malady: Women, Madness, and English Culture, 1830-1980* (1985; New York: Viking Penguin Inc., 1987).

3 Szasz, *Ideology and Insanity* 9-10.

4 Ralph Ellison, *Invisible Man* (1947; New York: Vintage Books, 1972) 568).

5 Ellen Morgan, "Humanbecoming: Form and Focus in the Neo-Feminist Novel", *Images of Women in Fiction*, ed. Susan Koppelman Cornillon (Bowling Green: Bowling Green University Popular Press, 1972) 185.

6 Elizabeth Abel, Marianne Hirsch, and Elizabeth Langland, eds. *The Voyage In: Fictions of Female Development* (Hanover, UP of New England, 1983) 5.

7 Abel, Hirsch, Langland 6-7.

8 Clara Thomas, "Mr. Rochester's First Marriage: *Wide Sargasso Sea* by Jean Rhys," *WLWE* 17 (1978): 350, 356. Thomas Staley also notes in his book *Jean Rhys: A Critical Study* (Austin: U of Texas P, 1979), that "Rhys's concentration is on the psychological, the personal traumas which historical events produce rather than on the events themselves" (103).

⁹ Elizabeth Nunez-Harrell, "The Paradoxes of Belonging: The White West Indian Woman in Fiction", *Modern Fiction Studies* 31 (1985): 281-282.

¹⁰ Bessie Head, *A Question of Power* (1974; London: Heinemann, 1985) 16. All subsequent references are to this edition.

¹¹ Jean Rhys, *Wide Sargasso Sea* (1966; Harmondsworth: Penguin, 1987) 40. All subsequent references are to this edition.

¹² Ezekiel Mphahlele, "The Tyrany of Place", *New Letters* 40 (1973) 70.

¹³ John Milton, *Paradise Lost*, ed. Merritt Y. Hughes (1962; Indianapolis: The Odyssey Press, 1981) 86 (IV 75). This idea is also echoed in Book IV when Militon describes Satan as he approaches Eden:
horror and doubt distract
His troubl'd thoughts, and from the bottom stir
The Hell within him, for within him Hell
He brings, and round about him, nor from Hell
One step no more than from himself can fly
By change of place
p. 84 (IV 18-23)

¹⁴ The only segment related by Antoinette in Part Two is that chronicling her visit to Christrophine, pp. 89-98.

¹⁵ Arnold E. Davidson, *Jean Rhys* (New York: Frederick Ungar, 1985) 29.

¹⁶ Rhys seems to engage here in a bit of metafiction. This reminder that there is always another side to every story is an appropriate one for this novel wherein Rhys sought to tell Berthat Rochester's story (*Jane Eyre*; Charlotte Bronte).

¹⁷ Marianne Hirsch, "Spiritual *Bildung*: The Beautiful Soul as Paradigm", *The Voyage In* 44. Hirsch maintains in this article that suicide in the female *bildungsroman* "is not neurotic but a realistic and paradoxically fulfilling reaction to an impossible contradiction."

¹⁸ Jennifer Waelti-Walters, *Fairy Tales and the Female Imagination* (Montreal: Eden Press, 1982) 89.

¹⁹ Charles Ponnuthurai Sarvan, "Bessie Head: *A Question of Power* and Identity", *Women in African Liteaturee Today* (London: James Currey, 1987) 82.

²⁰ According to Abel, Hirsch and Langland in *The Voyage In*, "the female protagonist or *Bildungsheld* must chart a treacherous course between the penalties of expressing sexuality and suppressing it" (12).

[21] Phyllis Chessler, *Women and Madness* (1972; New York: Avon, 1973) 36. Chesler notes that, "Celibacy is the official order of the asylum day. Patients are made to inhabit an eternal American adolescence, where sexuality and aggression are as feared, mocked and punished as they are within the Family."

[22] Linda Susan Beard, "Bessie Head in Gaborone, Botswana: An Interview", *Sage* III (1986): 45. In response to Beard's question, "Is Elizabeth Bessie?", Bessie Head states, "There's no way in which I can deny that that was a completely autobiographical novel taking a slice of my life, my experience, and transcribing it verbatim into novel form."

[23] Kolawole Ogungbesan, "The Cape Gooseberry Also Grows in Botswana: Alienation and Commitment in the Writings of Bessie Head", *Journal of African Studies* 6 (1979-1980): 211.

[24] Cecil A. Abrahams, "The Tyranny of Place: The Context of Bessie Head's Fiction", *WLWE* 17 (1978) 29.

The Politics of Madness in Bessie Head

Roger A. Berger

for it is not true that the work of man is done
that we have no business being on earth
that we parasite the world
that it is enough for us to heel to the world
whereas the work has only begun
and man still must overcome all the interdictions
    wedged in the recesses of his fervor and no race has
a monopoly on beauty, on intelligence, on strength

and there is room for everyone at the convocation
    of conquest

--Aime Cesaire
Notebook of a Return to the Native Land

I begin with this quotation from Cesaire because he was among the first to understand that nationalism and independence do not signify any kind of end point for the struggle for human liberation--that there exists, as Dennis Brutus tells us, "the much / that remains to be done." And I eventually want to return to this vision, because it has in the final analysis much to do with Bessie Head's perspective, as presented in *A Question of Power*, about what needs to be done to move the world beyond the nightmare of racism—of all varieties. But in the meantime, I want to discuss what strikes me as an anomaly found in the critical response to the novel, and employ that anomaly to suggest an alternative, radically historicized reading of the novel's meaning and significance.

The criticism of *A Question of Power*, that is to say, has been for the most part of excellent quality, explicating to a large degree what is to all extents and purposes an extraordinarily difficult text. It suggests in main how the novel concerns, in the context of apartheid, the question of evil—specifically in terms of interpersonal relationships, exploring "the sources of evil, [exposing] its true face, and [showing] the misery and suffering it inflicts on human life" (Pearse 87). As Bessie Head herself writes, "I argued [in *A Question of Power*] that people and nations do not realise the point at which they become evil but once trapped in its net, evil has a powerful propelling motion into a terrible abyss of destruction. I argued that its form, design, and plan could be clearly outlined and that it was little understood as a force in the affairs of mankind (Head, *WLWE* 24).

However, despite the excellence of the criticism on the text, it strikes me as strange that almost no one has remarked, so far as I can tell, on the fact that Elizabeth's objects of anxiety—the horrific projections that persecute her—are *black*.

Elizabeth, briefly to summarize the text, has exiled herself from the monstrous apartheid system of South Africa to the sparer yet seemingly saner country of Botswana, specifically to a small town called Motabeng. There, while she naturally is *not* accepted in every way—especially by the local Botswanan people—she nonetheless finds, in utter contrast to South Africa, warm, humane, caring people—from the Principal of the Motabeng Secondary School or Eugene, the politically committed head of the "local industries" project designed to free Botswana from reliance on South Africa, or Tom, the Peace Corps volunteer, to Kenosi, the Botswanan woman who works with Elizabeth on the village garden. To use the term of one critic, these people seem "raceless" in their commitment both to a nonracial society and to a nonexploitative economy (Heywood 16). We can see this communal sense represented in an early scene:

> People often looked at Elizabeth with a cheated air. She had been taught the greeting in Setswana up to the first five lines and had no delicious tidbits of gossip to offer. A person would actually put out her hand to stay her: 'Wait a bit Where are you hurrying to?' It was so new, so inconceivable, the extreme opposite of 'Hey Kaffir, get out of the way', the sort of greeting one usually was given in South Africa. (20-1)

Or later, when Eugene tells Elizabeth, "'We want to turn people's attention to their natural resources .... if people only knew how and what to use from their surroundings we could become independent of the goods of the rich manufacturers in South Africa and

Rhodesia'" (69), we understand the commitment by some of the people in the community to liberate themselves from South Africa's economic hegemony. Yet in spite of this kind environment, Elizabeth suffers *two* nervous breakdowns—which apparently isn't an unusual event as the Principal tells her that "'A lot of refugees have nervous breakdowns'" (52)—and the nightmare of these collapses manifests itself in the projections of Sello, Dan, Medusa and a host of other black personalities and visions. Most commentators correctly deduce the source of these nightmarish dreams in Elizabeth's oppressed situation in South Africa, where, as the child of a white woman (who eventually goes insane and commits suicide) and a black father, she finds herself utterly dislocated, the object of unbearable scorn from the white community. (See Abrahams) But it is strange, it seems to me, for Elizabeth to project her understandable neuroses in terms of two local black men, whom she barely knows, from the Motabeng village. If anything, one would expect that her projections and delusions—the brilliantly represented monsters of her dreams—would take the form of *whites*, if not the whites of South Africa, then at least, say, Camilla, the racist white woman Elizabeth comes to work with at the garden. Yet patently this is not the case. So, given the nature of her nightmares, it seems to me that we might reconfigure the cause and nature of Elizabeth's pathology not in terms of eurocentric psychoanalysis—which operates as the hermeneutic paradigm for previous readings of the text—but in terms of a decolonized psychopathology.

To reconfigure the etiology of her insanity, I suggest that we might look at Frantz Fanon's brilliant, early *Black Skin, White Masks*, in which he explains the inadequacy of eurocentric psychoanalysis (that is, specifically, of Freud and Jung) to the colonized and charts a different map of psychopathology—a radically historicized or politicized one—for people of color. Before I briefly adumbrate Fanon's argument, however, let me state that Fanon of course has his limitations, and he should not be applied in an unmediated way to *A Question of Power*. In the chapter I shall refer to, Fanon focuses mainly on white men and women and on black men, though he does interestingly conclude his discussion with an amazingly suggestive account of a neurotic Antillean woman; and though we would like to think, had he lived longer, that Fanon would have responded positively to the challenge of feminist literary and psychoanalytical theory (some suggestion towards this appears in *A Dying Colonialism*), we must admit nevertheless that black women (except in relation to white men) are curiously absent from Fanon's discussion and that this absence clearly calls upon us to temper our enthusiasm and application of the Fanon. Nonetheless, what he has to say about the problematics of ethnopsychiatry (which is, in essence, the imperialist wing of eurocentric psychoanalysis) and about the interesting situation of the Antillean black (especially as it relates to the dislocated condition of those of mixed parentage in South Africa) offers, I believe, much to consider in relation to Bessie Head's *A Question of Power*.

Fanon argues in his crucial chapter on "The Negro and Psychopathology" that while for whites there exists a clear analogy between the family and those subsequent institutions (like the State) that dominate and often make neurotic the adult—and hence, validating the Freudian paradigm for the European—the "normal Negro child ... will become abnormal on the slightest contact with the white world" (143). Thus, Fanon insists, it is the *colonial encounter*—not some supposedly universal Oedipus Complex—that accounts for the psychopathology of the black. As Fanon notes, the colonized's "every neurosis ... is the product of his cultural situation" (152). What often occurs, then, in this colonial situation—and if I might look ahead momentarily and suggest what Elizabeth endured *in* South Africa was (and continues to be) a colonial situation—is that the colonized person attempts to become white. "When the Negro makes contact with the white world," writes Fanon, "a certain sensitizing action takes place. If his psychic structure is weak, one observes a collapse of the ego. The black man stops behaving as an *actional* person. The goal of his behavior will be The Other (in the guise of the white man), for The Other alone can give him worth" (154). But that is not the whole story, for Fanon also understands that the black person is for Europeans especially in the Jungian *collective unconscious—"the symbol of Evil* ... the torturer is the black man, Satan is black, one talks of shadows, when one is dirty one is black—then one is thinking of physical dirtiness or of moral dirtiness" (189). Thus, because the black internalizes this worldview—or an Fanon states, "Through the collective unconscious the Antillean has taken over all the archtypes belonging to the European" (191)—"The negro selects for himself as an object capable of carrying the burden of original sin. The white man chooses the black man for this function, and the black man who is white also chooses the black man. The black Antillean is the slave of this cultural imposition. After having been the slave of the white man, he enslaves himself. The Negro is in every sense of the word a victim of white civilization" (192). As I suggested before, Fanon then ends this chapter by offering a case study of a black woman who because she has assimilated the "myth of the Negro [or] fear of the Negro" has been suffering from an inability to function very similar to the breakdowns that torment Elizabeth. To summarize, then, colonial psychopathology, according to Fanon, assumes two forms: the black desires the prohibited Otherness of the white and, simultaneously, accepts the race fantasy image of him or herself.

This model offers a more internally and politically coherent psychoanalytical explanation for Elizabeth's pathology *and thus can* help us understand precisely what the text suggests about the process of decolonization that must be endured to liberate the self from the race fantasies imposed by the white regime in South Africa. It is the colonial encounter with the whites—and in particular, Elizabeth's internalizing the race fantasies of the white South African hegemonic regime—that serves as the origin (or what Freud termed the "traumatic neurosis" [*Introductory Lectures* 275]) of her psychopathology. This trauma locates its origin not in the Freudian family romance but first in the general condition of apartheid and then in the specific confrontation with the white. Bessie Head dramatizes these general and specific confrontations in the early part of the novel. For example, Head tells us that Elizabeth, who has grown up with a foster-mother is "secretly relieved to be taken away from the beer-house [that the foster-mother is reduced to operating] and sent to a mission school, as hours and hours of her childhood had been spent sitting under a lamp-post near her house, crying because everyone was drunk and there was no food, no one to think about children" (15-6). This represents clearly the systemic material and psychological deprivation created by apartheid, and as Head makes clear, Elizabeth "lived the back-breaking life of all black people in South Africa. It was like living with *permanent nervous tension* because you did not know why white people there had to go out of their way to hate you or loathe you. They were just born that way, hating people, and a black man or woman was just born to be hated. There wasn't any lift to the heart, just this vehement vicious struggle between two sets of people with different looks" (19, emphasis added). Everyday life in South Africa, conditioned as it is by this "permanent nervous tension," thus exemplifies a colonial psychopathology.

But the text also represents a specific colonial encounter, which serves as the traumatizing experience for Elizabeth. After she arrives at the mission school, Elizabeth encounters "The principal of the mission school" who is described as "a tall, thin, gaunt, incredibly cruel woman." As Head continues,

> She was the last, possibly, of the kind who had
> heard 'the call' from Jesus and come out to save the
> heathen. Their calls seemed to make them very
> bitter at the end of it, and their professed love for
> Jesus never awakened love and compassion in
> their hearts. As soon as Elizabeth arrived at the
> mission school, she was called to one side by the
> principal and given the most astounding informa-
> tion. She said:
>   'We have a full docket on you. You must be
> very careful. Your mother was insane. If you're
> not careful you'll get insane just like your mother.
> Your mother was a white woman. They had to
> lock her up, as she was having a child by the stable
> boy, who was a native.' (16).

This key passage, which assumes for Elizabeth the status of a
master narrative, must be framed by what we know about apartheid and what we have learned about the corruption or misuse of
psychoanalysis as outlined by Fanon. Textual evidence exists, first
of all, to suggest that Elizabeth's mother was not "insane": there is,
to begin, something in one of her mother's letters that asks the
mission to "'Please set aside some money for my child's education
....'" (16, Head's elipses) that suggests some level of lucidity, and it
is clear, given the draconian measures against miscegenation in
South Africa, that any inter-racial intimacy is construed by the
whites as "insane". We must now allow ourselves to interpret
behavior according to the monstrous "logic" of apartheid. Indeed,
the fact that her mother committed suicide after six years of
institutionalization suggests at best the hopelessness—*not* the insanity—she must have experienced; and of course, we can only
speculate on the tragic fate meted out to the father.

However, most important is *not* the white insistence of his
mother's madness; rather what is most troubling is Elizabeth's
internalizing the race fantasy that insanity is in some way *hereditary*.
It must be made clear immediately that hereditary insanity, along
with the other myths of ethnopsychiatry (e.g., the savagery of the
native, his or her innate childishness) that Fanon explicitly ex-
plodes in *The Wretched of the Earth*, has no basis in reality and reflects
merely the extension of racism into psychoanalysis. Unfortunately,
Elizabeth eventually accepts this myth as ontologically given. At
first, Head tells us, Elizabeth "could not relate to [the story of her
mother's incarceration] in any way. She really belonged emotion-

ally to her foster-mother, and the story was an imposition on her life" (16). However, the same was "Not so for the missionary. She lived on the alert for Elizabeth's insanity" (16). And so, this race fantasy affects Elizabeth first physically and eventually psychologically:

> Once Elizabeth struck a child during a quarrel and the missionary ordered:
> 'Isolate her from the other children for a week.'
> The other children soon noticed something unusual about Elizabeth's isolation periods. They could fight and scratch and bite each other, but if she did likewise she was locked up. They took to kicking at her with deliberate malice as she sat in a corner reading a book. None of the prefects would listen to her side of the story.
> 'Come on', they said, 'The principal said you must be locked up.'
> At the time, she had merely hated the principal with a *black*, deep bitter rage. But later, when she became aware of subconscious appeals to share love, to share suffering, she wondered if the persecution had been so much the outcome of the principal's twisted version of life as *the silent appeal* of her dead mother:
> 'Now you know. Do you think I can bear the stigma of insanity alone? Share it with me.' (16-7, emphasis mine)

In *Black Skin, White Masks*, Fanon explains clearly that in the colonial encounter the black child is generally denied the same cathartic outlets as other children, and this scene clearly reenacts that trauma. It is equally important to note that Elizabeth's anger is at first "black" and potentially revolutionary; however, afterwards, she internalizes the race fantasy of hereditary insanity (understandably, of course, given her torture at the hands of the racist principal) and *fantasizes* a request from her mother to share her insanity. We must not forget that she responds to what Bessie Head terms "the silent appeal of her dead mother." No textual evidence exists, that is to say, that Elizabeth's mother ever explicitly articulated such a request. Rather, Elizabeth assimilates the missionary's theory about insanity and then proceeds, when she is confronted with the "raceless" world of Botswana, to go mad:

> One might propose an argument, then, with the
> barriers of the normal, conventional and sane all
> broken down, like a swimmer taking a rough
> journey on wild seas. It was in Botswana where
> mentally, the normal and the abnormal blended
> completely in Elizabeth's mind. It was manage-
> able to a certain point because of Elizabeth's back-
> ground and the freedom and flexibility with which
> she brought herself up. Was the story of her
> mother sheer accident or design? It seemed to add
> to her temperament and capacity to endure the
> excruciating. (15)

In Fanonist terms, then, it should not be surprising that
Elizabeth, having accepted the white version of reality, imagines
her psychopathological state not in terms of the whites but through
the black community she believes rejects her. And her acceptance
of the white fantasy of inherited insanity manifests itself clearly in
terms of the way she *represents* her terrifying projections. In
contrast to other readings—one seeing the two major black projections, Sello and Dan, as competing systems for confronting evil
(Johnson), another interpreting them as representing the subcon-
scious and the unconscious (Pearse)—I want to suggest that these
hideous projections are in the final analysis indeterminant. Indeed,
it is their indeterminancy that gives them their terrifying power:
placing them within a Freudian paradigm serves merely to domes-
ticate them. Yet their often moving representations do have some
consistency: they embody certain racist myths (the native as overly
sexualized or the native as irrational and so on). It is significant, to
take but one example, that Elizabeth is endlessly threatened by
their sexual prowess, as we can see in this scene with Dan:

> The next night [Dan] introduced a girl. She had
> her hair done up in the traditional style; small
> chunks of hair were tied on to a length of string
> and wound round and round the head. The girl
> bowed her head so that Elizabeth could get a good
> look at her hair-do. Dan said:
>   'I like girls like this with that kind of hair.
> Your hair is not properly African.'

She wasn't the usual sort of girl. She was a specialist in sex. A symbol went hand in hand with her, a small sewing machine with a handle.

'She can go with a man the whole night and feel no ill-effects the next day, provided you stimulate her properly', Dan explained.

The stimulation worked like a sewing machine; turn the handle with a big swing, then the needle rattles up and down; turn the handle again and so on. It looked as if the key to it was her penny-button. She liked her penny-button tickled.

His other comment on Miss Sewing-Machine was: 'She's a demon of self-control.'

Then he simply tumbled the girl into bed beside Elizabeth and went with her the whole night. The lights on the cinema screen of her mind were down, but not their activity. They kept on bumping her awake till at dawn they made the last bump, bump, bump.

He pressed several buttons at the same time:
You are supposed to feel jealous.
You are inferior as a Coloured.
You haven't got what that girl has got. (126-7)

This scene represents the race fantasies (about native sexuality and about race distinctions) that Elizabeth has accepted as true, and terrifying weds Elizabeth's psychosexual and racial anxieties. It thus offers strong evidence for reading these representations not in terms of some Freudian or Existential category but as reflecting the hegemony of a colonial psychopathology.

Bessie Head offers in *A Question of Power* a provisional "solution" to this colonial psychopathology. Elizabeth can "cure" herself of her madness only when she returns to the land and, through the help of the peasants, she reconceives a global humanist vision. Here Fanon once again serves as a guide. As Fanon tells us in *The Wretched of the Earth*, "the *fellah*, the unemployed man, the starving native do not lay claim to the truth; they do not *say* that they represent the truth, for they *are* the truth" (49). Similarly, we read in Bessie Head that in response to a presentation made by the "local-industries: self-help program, "the cynical-eyed villagers listened to all these explanations of productivity with reserve. They were the last people on earth to be told about how to work and produce things with their own hands; they did it all the time. They gathered the earth together and built it up into solid walls of mud for their homes; they felled trees in the bush for the supports of rafters of their roofs and cut the long, rough wild grass for their thatch. They know about living on nothing" (153). Elizabeth must embrace the "fearlessness" of the peasant and with them reclaim the land, which is, to Fanon, what the colonial struggle is ultimately all about. Through her work on the garden, Elizabeth is able to connect her knowledge of the land to a general understanding of evil and a vision of a non-exploitative future for all of humankind:

> 'There's some such thing as black people's suffering being a summary of everything the philosophers and prophets ever said', she said. "They said: "Never think along the lines of I and mine. It is death." But they said it prettily, under the shade of Bodhi trees. It made no impact on mankind in general. It was for an exclusive circle of followers. Black people learned that lesson brutally because they were the living victims of the greed inspired by I and mine and to hell with you, dog. Where do you think their souls are, then, after centuries of suffering? They're ahead of Buddha and Jesus and can dictate the terms for the future, not for any exclusive circle but for mankind in general .... Africa isn't rising. It's up already. It depends on where one places the stress. I place it on the soul. If it's basically right there, then other things fall into place. That's my struggle, and that's black power, but it's a power that belongs to all of mankind and in which all mankind can share. (134-5)

This is Cesaire's vision, which I quoted at the beginning of this essay, and we can see a similar vision in Fanon—in *Black Skin, White Masks* and in *The Wretched of the Earth*—that imagines the liberation of people of color and, most important, of all humankind:

> I, man of color want only this:
> That the tool never possess the man. That the enslavement of man by man cease forever. That is, of one by another. That it be possible for me to discover and to love man, where he may be.

> The Negro is not. Any more than the white
> man.
>
> Both must turn their backs on the inhuman
> voices which were those of their respective ances-
> tors in order that authentic communication be
> possible. Before it can adopt a positive voice,
> freedom requires an effort at disalienation .... It is
> through the effort to recapture the self and to
> scrutinize the self, it is through the lasting tension
> of their freedom that men will be able to create the
> ideal conditions of existence for a human world.
> (231)

This magnificently human statement from *Black Skin, White Masks* resonates with what we find in *A Question of Power* when Elizabeth early on discovers "that no one was the be-all and end-all of creation, that no one had the power of assertion and dominance to the exclusion of other life ... that people, in their souls, were forces, energies, stars, planets, universes and all kinds of swirling magic and mystery ... an awakening of her own powers corresponded to an awakening love of mankind" (35). This vision offers, as we read near the end of the novel, "a kind of liberation ... and a new dawn and a new world. She felt this because the basic error seemed to be a relegation of all things holy to some unseen Being in the sky. Since man was not holy to man, he could be tortured for his complexion, he could be misused, degraded and killed. If there were any revelation whatsoever in her own suffering it seemed to be quite the reverse of Mohammed's dramatic statement. She said: there is only one God and his name is Allah. And Mohammed is his prophet. She said: there is only one God and his name is Man. And Elizabeth is his prophet" (205-6). This encapsulates Bessie Head's radically secular utopian vision, a vision that emerges dramatically from a triumph over the psychopathological nightmare of coloni-alism.

Bessie Head's *A Question of Power* does not, of course, repli-cate completely Fanon's notions on colonial psychopathology. But her text offers an intriguing extension of Fanon's paradigm, be-cause the novel's protagonist, like Bessie Head herself, has experienced *both* a colonial and a neocolonial world. The novel, then, chronicles Elizabeth's courageous quest to rid herself of the pathology of apartheid and to reconstitute herself as an historical subject. "[I]n Africa," Bessie Head concludes her novel, "She had fallen from the very beginning into the warm embrace of the brotherhood of man, because when a people wanted everyone to be ordinary it was just another way of saying man loved man. As she fell asleep, she placed one soft hand over her land. It was a gesture of belonging" (206). Elizabeth indeed triumphs over the forces designed to imprison her, but it is not a victory of reconciliation with her Freudian neuroses, nor is it a narrative embodying a universal existential psychoanalysis; rather she conquers the psychopathology of the colonial encounter. It is at the end a political triumph understood through the "power that belongs to all of mankind and in which all mankind can share" (135).

Notes

[1] See, for example, Abrahams, Beard, Heywood, Johnson, Ogungbesan, and Pearse.

[2] See Pearse to whose article I am greatly indebted, even though we have great differences. For example, Pearse notes that "Bessie Head's narrator undermines [the] argument of hereditary insanity by exposing the society's prejudicial treatment of Elizabeth, and by emphasizing the social background to Elizabeth's mother's supposed insanity" (82). Yet Pearse also argues that "Bessie Head structures Elizabeth's madness along the lines of basic existential psychoanalysis" (88), suggesting a kind of universal psychopathology, which, I shall argue, the test subverts.

Works Cited

Abrahams, Cecil. "The Tyranny of Place: The Context of Bessie Head's Fiction", *WLWE* 17.1 (1978): 30-37.

Beard, Linda Susan. "Bessie Head's *A Question of Power*: The Journey Through Disintegration to Wholeness", *Colby Library Quarterly* 15.4 (1979): 267-274.

Cesaire, Aime. *The Collected Poetry*, trans. Clayton Eshlman and Annette Smith. Berkeley: California UP, 1983.

Fanon, Frantz. *Black Skin, White Masks*, trans. Charles Markmann. NY: Grove, 1967.

—. *The Wretched of the Earth*, trans. Constance Farrington. NY: Grove, 1961.

Freud, Sigmund. *Introductory Lectures on Psychoanalysis*. NY: Liveright, 1966.

Head, Bessie. *A Question of Power*. London: Heinemann, 1974.

—. "Social and Political Pressures That Shape Literature in Southern Africa", *WLWE* 18.1 (1979): 20-26.

Heywood, Christopher. "Traditional Values in the Novels of Bessie Head", *Individual and Community in Commonwealth Literature*. Ed. Daniel Massa. Malta: University Press, 1979: 12-19.

Johnson, Joyce. "Metaphor, Myth and Meaning in Bessie Head's *A Question of Power*", *WLWE* 25.2 (1985): 198-211.

Ogungbesan, Kolawole. "The Cape Gooseberry Also Grows in Botswana: Alienation and Commitment in the Writings of Bessie Head", *Journal of African Studies* 6.4 (1979-80): 206-212.

Pearse, Adetokunbo. "Apartheid and Madness: Bessie Head's *A Question of Power*", *Kunapipi* 5.2 (1983): 81-98.

Venturing into Feminist Consciousness

Nancy Topping Bazin

Media reports about international women's meetings and even sessions at the National Women's Studies Association conferences too often perpetuate the myth that third world women hold women's issues in low priority. It is important, therefore, to note that two of the best novels by contemporary Black African women writers focus upon the growing feminist consciousness of their protagonists. Nnu Ego in Buchi Emecheta's *The Joys of Motherhood* (1979) and Elizabeth in Bessie Head's *A Question of Power* (1974) both move away from innocence into an understanding of the patriarchal culture in which they live. They gain this understanding through experiences so overwhelming and horrifying that each woman barely survives. However, the two protagonists emerge from their ventures with strength, wisdom, and clarity of vision they did not previously possess.

Buchi Emecheta's *The Joys of Motherhood* illuminates brilliantly the meaning of Adrienne Rich's concept, "the institution of motherhood."[1] Although the general public rarely perceives the distinction, feminists are not against biological motherhood but they are against what Rich describes—namely, the patriarchal use of motherhood to keep women relatively powerless. Buchi Emecheta's novel begins with Nnu Ego, in a state of despair, running blindly towards the river to drown herself. Nnu Ego has already lost one husband because she did not become pregnant, and the son she had born for her second husband has just died. At this point Nnu Ego attempts suicide because, when pain and anger rose inside of her, "sometimes anger came to the fore, but the emotional pain always won."[2] By the end of the book, her consciousness allows the anger to dominate the pain, thereby giving her the power to act and to choose rather than simply to suffer. Like Elizabeth in Bessie Head's *A Question of Power*, Nnu Ego never achieves much freedom. However, anger has forced her to analyze the situation of women, thus giving her the basis for wiser decisions.

Buchi Emecheta frequently uses African belief systems to provide the framework for her story.[3] In *The Joys of Motherhood*, Nnu Ego's initial infertility is said to be the revengeful work of her father's slave girl who became understandably angry when she was told she must accept the custom of being buried alive with her dead mistress. Although "a good slave was supposed to jump into the grave willingly", even happily, this slave had to be killed to make her lie still (p. 23). To free Nnu Ego from the young slave woman's curse, the father frees all his slaves (p. 35). Longing so for the baby required by the community, Nnu Ego dreams that a baby boy is offered to her; as she wades across a stream to get it, the slave woman laughs mockingly at her and the water rises so she cannot reach the baby. Ironically, she is glorified after her death by a shrine, and she herself has become the woman in the other world who denies fertility to young wives: "however many people appealed to her to make women fertile, she never did!" (p. 224). She denies them fertility, however, not like the slave woman, to be vengeful, but rather to save them from the fate she had known. The change from weeping because she is childless, to anger because she spent the rest of her life bearing nine children and caring for the seven who lived, is the consequence of the feminist consciousness she has acquired through her experiences.

Nnu Ego has long been aware of the cruel treatment women received from men. In her flight towards suicide, she recalls the tales of her father's polygamous behavior. He had at his disposal seven wives and two mistresses. He flaunted his favoritism for one of the two mistresses, Nnu Ego's mother by noisily making love to her in the courtyard so all his neglected wives could hear. To dominate even this favorite, the father tried to reduce her "to longing and craving for him", to humiliate her "in her burning desire" (p. 20). This courtyard behavior caused his first wife to have a seizure and die (p. 22).

Nnu Ego also learned about patriarchal attitudes through her experiences with her first husband. When she does not become pregnant, she masochistically takes the blame: "I am sure the fault is on my side. You do everything right." (p. 31). But he feels free to make this cruel statement: "I have no time to waste my precious male seed on a woman who is infertile" (p. 32). Soon he takes a second wife who becomes pregnant the first month. The husband tells Nnu Ego: "I will do my duty by you. I will come to your hut when my wife starts nursing her child. But now, if you can't produce sons, at least you can help harvest yams" (p. 33). Such male behavior was usual; therefore, although Nnu Ego suffers, she continues to blame only herself for her pain.

Nnu Ego's education in the ways of the patriarch continues as her father buys her back from her first husband and sells her to another family. In each case, the bride price changes hands between the males. Although Nnu Ego finds herself in Lagos with an ugly, fat husband whom neither she nor her father had met, she feels she must accept the situation because the chief concern of her family back in Ibuza is that she get pregnant. She knows they will not tolerate any rebellion on her part. When she receives a message from home, it is, "Your big mother said I should tell your husband to hurry up and do his work because her arms are itching for a baby to rock" (p. 76). Given this kind of pressure from the family, her reaction to pregnancy is not surprising: "He has made me into a real woman—all I want to be, a woman and a mother" (p. 53). Although that first baby dies, she goes on to have two sons, Oshia and Adim. At times she is extremely miserable in the marriage, when her husband inherits his dead brother's wives and brings one home to live with them. But still she cannot protest for her father would say:

> "Why do you want to stand in your husband's way? Please don't disgrace the name of the family again. What greater honour is there for a woman than to be a mother, and now you are a mother— not of daughters who will marry and go, but of good-looking healthy sons, and they are the first sons of your husband and you are his first and senior wife. Why do you wish to behave like a woman brought up in a poor household? (p. 119)

Even when she goes back for her father's funeral, she knows that people will soon say, "You have already proved you are a good daughter, but a good daughter must also be a good wife" (p. 155). Her roles of daughter, wife, and mother are rigidly defined and she is expected to fulfill them according to custom for, in her husband's words, "What else does a woman want?" (p. 49).

In addition to fulfilling her roles, which includes almost constant pregnancy, the two customs that cause Nnu Ego to suffer are the practices of polygamy and son preference. Her husband Nnaife's attitude was: "If a woman cared for him, very good; if not, there would always be another who would care" (p. 95). When the second wife, Adaku, comes into their home, Nnu Ego observes: "Strange how in less than five hours Nnaife had become a rare commodity" (p. 121). She has to prepare her bed for Nnaife and Adaku and at night has to listen to their love-making. She tried to block her ears, yet could still hear Adaku's exaggerated carrying on. Nnu Ego tossed in agony and anger all night, going through in her imagination what was taking place behind the curtained bed (p. 124). On Nnaife's first night home after the war, Nnu Ego endured his public declaration that he must go to Ibuza to see another wife, Adankwo, inherited from his dead brother. He makes all the male visitors laugh by saying, "She must be longing for a man. For a woman to be without a man for five years! My brother will never forgive me" (p. 182). Although Nnu Ego becomes pregnant once again, he still visits Adankwo and gives her her "last menopausal baby" (p. 183). However, she will not go back to Lagos with him, so he pays the expectionally high price of thirty pounds to bring home a sixteen-year-old bride (p. 184). Nnu Ego, who is expecting twins, screams at him, "We only have one room to share with my five children, and I'm expecting another two, yet you have brought another person. Have you been commissioned by the white people you fought for to replace those dead during the war?" (p. 184). Yet a neighbour quiets her by saying, "Your father would not be happy to see you behave this way." She does not think for herself, for "even in death Nwokocha Agbadi ruled his daughter. She belonged to both men, her father and her husband, and lastly to her sons. Yes, she would have to be careful if she did not want her sons' future wives to say, "But your mother was always jealous whenever her husband brought home a young wife" (p. 185).

Nnu Ego accepts for a long time the patriarchal attitude that sons are much more valuable than daughters. When she bears twin girls, she feels ashamed. Her worst fears are realized when their father looks at them and says, "Nnu Ego, what are these? Could you not have done better? Where will we all sleep, eh? What will they eat?" (p. 127). Her co-wife Adaku consoles her by saying: "It's a man's world this. Still, senior wife, these girls when they grow up will be great helpers to you in looking after the boys. Their bride prices will be used in paying their school fees as well" (p. 127). Adaku herself is not respected because she has no male children. But ironically, the female loses either way. Simply because Nnu Ego was "the mother of three sons, she was supposed to be happy in her poverty, in her nail-biting agony, in her churning stomach, in her rags, in her cramped room .... Oh, it was a confusing world" (p. 167). When Adaku loses a baby boy, she goes into deep depression. As Nnu Ego's son Oshia tries to console her by saying she still has her daughter Dumbi, Adaku snaps back, "You are worth more than ten Dumbis." From then on, Oshia realizes his superior status; he refuses to fetch water or help cook because "That's a woman's job." This behavior is excused by the community as being "just like a boy" (p. 128).

Nnu Ego follows the custom of expecting boys to get much more education than girls. Her daughters go to school for only a couple of years and, even at that, they must do petty trading after school; "the boys, on the other hand were encouraged to put more time into their school work" (p. 180). Nnu Ego tells her girls that they must do this work to raise money to educate the boys and "put them in a good position in life, so that they will be able to look after the family." The mother cites the reward for the girls: "When your husbands are nasty to you, they will defend you" (p. 176).

As Nnu Ego participates in the patriarchal system both as victim and as perpetrator of it, she is angry more and more frequently. She realizes more and more clearly that the institution of motherhood has greatly limited her freedom and power. When Nnaife gives his wives too little money for food, Nnu Ego finds that, because her children might starve if he becomes angry, her power to struggle against him is minimal:

> "She was a prisoner, imprisoned by her love for her children, imprisoned in her role as the senior wife. She was not even expected to demand more money for her family; that was considered below the standard expected of a woman in her positiion. It was not fair, the way men cleverly used a woman's sense of responsibility to actually enslave her" (p. 137).

Growing more and more rebellious, she asks, "God, when will you create a woman who will be fulfilled in herself, a full human being, not anybody's appendage?" She laments: "What have I gained from all this? Yes, I have many children, but what do I feed them on? On my life. I have to work myself to the bone to look after them" (p. 186). Even after her death, they will worship her dead spirit, and if things do not go well, they will blame her. In desperation she asks "When will I be free?" (p. 187).

Finally, through her experiences with her father, husbands, and sons, she has come to understand the patriarchal nature of her culture and her own role in perpetuating it:

> "The men make it look as if we must aspire for
> children or die. That's why when I lost my first son
> I wanted to die, because I failed to live up to the
> standard expected of me by the males in my life,
> my father and my husband—and now I have to
> include my sons. But who made the law that we
> should not hope in our daughters? We women
> subscribe to that law more than anyone. Until we
> change all this, it is still a man's world, which
> women will always help to build" (p. 187)

Moreover, when Nnaife is proud of his sons, they are his children;
but when they fail to meet his expectations, they are her children.
Nnu Ego became fed up with "this two-way standard" (p. 206).

But Nnu Ego has awakened too late; she says at the end of the
book, "I don't know how to be anything else but a mother" (p. 222).
She has also recognized too late a fact that is evident to the reader
all through the book—male and female perspectives are very far
apart. Her drunken husband Nnaife tried to kill a potential son-in-
law because he was from the wrong tribe, so he is put in jail. Her
sons whom she expected to care for her in her old age are university
students who neither write nor send money. The reality of her life
is contrasted with the views of a man who is driving back to her
home village:

> "This life is very unfair for us men. We do all the
> work, you women take all the glory. You even live
> longer to reap the rewards. A son in America?
> You must be very rich, and I'm sure your husband
> is dead long ago ..."
> She did not think it worth her while to reply
> to this driver, who preferred to live in his world of
> dreams rather than face reality. What a shock he
> would have if she told him that her husband was
> in prison, or that the so-called son in America had
> never written to her directly, to say nothing of
> sending her money. If she should tell him that, he
> would look down on her and say, "But you're
> above all that, madam." (p. 223).

Nnu Ego's experiences have made her realize that women
must work together to "change all this" (p. 187). Nnu Ego has
ventured into feminist consciousness, but it is not until after her

death that she is free to take action by denying fertility to the young women. She knows that the continuous pressure to bear sons that drives them to her shrine will enslave them as it did her. Freedom for them must begin with rejecting the patriarchal glorification of motherhood.

Nnu Ego's journey into feminist consciousness is through marriage and motherhood. Bessie Head's protagonist in *A Question of Power* arrives at the same destination through a bout of madness. In her mad nightmare world, Elizabeth struggles against and survives patriarchal efforts to manipulate her spiritual and sexual being. She is able to regain her sanity only by recognizing that she must not respond passively to those who wish to dominate her. But Bessie Head's protagonist goes beyond the rejection of domination as a principle that determines attitudes and behavior to the articulation of an egalitarian philosophy. Whereas Buchi Emecheta's focus is upon personal experiences and social customs in a patriarchal African culture, Bessie Head's concern is with the spiritual or philosophical significance of patriarchal behavior.

The title *A Question of Power* clarifies further what this novel is about.[4] To Bessie Head whose daily life was shaped by the racist practices of South Africa and the sexist attitudes of the men she lived with, the question of who has the power is indeed important. Like Virginia Woolf, Zora Neale Hurston, and Doris Lessing, Bessie Head views the need of the male to see himself twice as big as he really is as one of the chief causes of unjust, undemocratic, and unkind behavior. In *A Question of Power* the male need to dominate and feel superior to others is represented by two men, Sello and Dan. They come to life and into power through the mad imaginings of Elizabeth. They are so real to her that she talks with them and feels her life literally threatened by them. It is because Sello and Dan use every power they have to try to destroy Elizabeth psychologically that she is mad. To regain her sanity, she must defeat them.

Elizabeth learns that Sello has already "killed several women", and he has molested his own child.[5] Moreover, he is the creator of the powerful Medusa, who inhabits Elizabeth's mad world. His Medusa is really "the direct and tangible form of his own evils, his power lusts, his greeds, his self importance" (p. 40). Medusa, manipulated by Sello, tortures Elizabeth until she almost obliterates her: "It wasn't Elizabeth's body she was thrusting into extinction. It was the soul; the bolts were aimed at her soul. It seemed to make death that much slower, that much more piece-meal. The narrow, mean eyes of Sello in the brown suit stared at her over Medusa's shoulder" (p. 87).

Sello and Dan try to kill Elizabeth's spirit. They do this primarily through manipulating her feelings about sexuality and through using sexuality to degrade her. To undermine Elizabeth's sense of herself as a woman, Sello uses Medusa, and Dan uses his "seventy-one nice-time girls" (p. 173). Medusa with a smile offers Elizabeth some secret information:

> It was about her vagina. Without any bother for decencies she sprawled her long black legs in the air, and the most exquisite sensation travelled out of her towards Elizabeth. It enveloped from head to toe like a slow, deep, sensuous bomb. It was like falling into deep, warm waters, lazily raising one hand and resting in a heaven of bliss. Then she looked at Elizabeth and smiled, a mocking superior smile: You haven't got anything *near* that, have you?" (p. 44).

Sello displays before Elizabeth his own attraction to Medusa. He "issued a low moan of anguish. He seemed to be desperately attached to that thing Medusa had which no other woman had. And even this was a mockery. It was abnormally constructed, like seven thousand vaginas in one, turned on and operating at white heat" (p. 64).

Elizabeth is attracted to Dan's overwhelming masculinity: "He made a woman feel like an ancient and knowledgeable queen of love" (0. 106). But Dan displays his power not just over her but over all women. He sadistically parades his many women before her and his message to her is that she should be jealous: "I go with all these women because you are inferior. You cannot make it up to my level." But, of course, just at the moment when she decides she dislikes him and wants "to pull her mind out of the chaos", he says: "If you leave me I'll die, because I have nothing else" (p. 147).

One of the key images in Elizabeth's madness is Dan "standing in front of her, his pants down, as usual, flaying his powerful penis in the air saying: "Look, I'm going to show you how I sleep with B ... She has a womb I can't forget. When I go with a woman I go for one hour. You can't do that" (pp. 12-13). His women include Miss Wriggly-Bottom, who "has small round breasts and a neat, nipped-in waist. She walked in time to a silent jazz tune she was humming and wriggled and wriggled her bottom" (p. 129). There was also Miss Sewing Machine who "liked her penny-button tickled" (p. 127). He added to the display "Miss Pelican-Beak, Miss Chopper, Miss Pink Sugar-Icing, whom he was on the point of marrying, Madame Make-Lone-On-The-Floor where anything goes, The Sugar-Plum Fairy, more of Body Beautiful, more of The Womb, a demonstration of sexual stamina with five local women, this time the lights on, Madame Squelch Squelch, Madame Loose-Bottom— the list of them was endless" (p. 148). Elizabeth took heavy doses of sleeping tablets to block out his all night activities with these "nice-time girls". For Dan sometimes tumbled these women into bed right beside Elizabeth ("They kept on bumping her awake"), and he encouraged them to use her personal possessions to clean up: "He was abnormally obsessed with dirt on his women. They washed and washed in her bathroom; they put on Elizabeth's dresses and underwear and made use of her perfumes" (pp. 127- 128).

Of course, if Dan finds that any of his seventy-one "nice-time girls" are too sexual, then he panics and turns against them. He views women as dirty if they are more sexually potent than he. He could not stand the sexual potency of Madame Loose-Bottom or the hysterical, feverish orgasm of Body Beautiful. Because the pelvis of Madame Squelch Squelch was like "molten lava", going with her made him throw up (pp. 164-165). One night he decided Miss Pelican-Beak with her long, tough vagina was "too pushy," so he broke her legs and elbows and redesigned her pelvis to make it more passive (pp. 167-168). Then he left her for Miss Chopped. Thus, his hatred for women was not all directed at Elizabeth. But she takes his behavior personally: "Why, why, why? What have I done?" Indeed it drives her further into madness; she becomes dysfunctional and must be hospitalized (pp. 173, 176).

Both Sello and Dan use male homosexuality to make Eliza- beth feel excluded. Dan tells Elizabeth it is a "universal phenome- non" (p. 138). He makes Sello appear before her with his boyfriend (p. 148), and he says, "They do it all the time" (p. 139). The displays of homosexuality like the displays of heterosexuality are meant to degrade her. These nightmares are extensions of her experiences with her husband: "Women were always complaining of being molested by her husband. Then there was also a white man who was his boy friend. After a year she picked up the small boy and walked out of the house, never to return" (p. 19).

Elizabeth's recognition of the similarity between racist and sexist attitudes is clear. She knew that white people "went out of their way to hate you or loathe you" (p. 19); similarly, Dan hits her with a "torrent of hatred" every day (p. 168). She finds the misogyny of some African males to be untempered by "love and tenderness and personal romantic treasuring of women" (p. 137). She calls both racists and sexists power-maniacs. "What did they gain, the power people, while they lived off other people's souls like vultures?" (p. 19). Medusa serves as an image for domination; she represents these attitudes: "Who's running the show around here? I am. Who knows everything around here? I do. Who's wearing the pants in this house? I am" (p. 43).

On a philosophical level, Elizabeth is saved from permanent madness by her faith in a value system different from Dan's and Sello's and by a different concept of God. In practice, she is saved by working in a garden with a woman friend Kenosi, who admires and respects her. Her work relationship with this woman provides her with a feminist model. Ultimately, Elizabeth rejects the patriarchal model of thinking and behaving in favor of a feminist mode of thinking and behaving. This rejection of a philosopy of domination in favor of an egalitarian philosophy is reflected in her comments about God.

Elizabeth rejects a god in the sky, because "God in heaven is too important to be decent" (p. 197). Her ideal is to bring holiness down to earth. The gods are, in fact, those "killed and killed and killed again in one cause after another for the liberation of mankind." She saw the gods as "ordinary, practical, sane people, seemingly their only distinction being that they had consciously concentrated on spiritual earnings. All the push and direction was towards the equality of man in his soul, as though, if it were not fixed up there, it never would be anywhere else." She concludes that "there are several hundred thousand people who are God" (p. 31). Her prayer is, "Oh God ... May I never contribute to creating dead worlds, only new worlds" (p. 100).

Elizabeth concludes that this can occur only through a struggle against greed and arrogance and an excessive concern for self (p. 134). Sello admits, "I thought too much of myself. I am the root cause of human suffering" (p. 36). At one point Elizabeth and Sello "perfected together the ideal of sharing everything and then perfectly shared everything with all mankind" (p. 202). But it is through the horrors of her contract with Dan in her hallucinations that she has learned the most:

> He had deepened and intensified all her qualities
> ... he taught by default—he taught iron and steel
> self-control through sheer, wild, abandoned de-
> bauchery; he taught the extremes of love and

tenderness through the extreme of hate; he taught
an alertness for falsehoods within, because he had
used any means at his disposal to destroy Sello.
And from the degradation and destruction of her
life had arisen a still, lofty serenity of soul nothing
could shake. (p. 202)

The aim must be to tap into one's powers, and she places her
emphasis on the soul: "If it's basically right there, then other things
fall into place. That's my struggle; and that's black power, but it's
a power that belongs to all mankind and in which all mankind can
share" (p. 135).

Although her language is sometimes sexist, Bessie Head's
philosopy and ethics parallel those of feminist philosopher/theo-
logians such as Rosemary Reuther, Naomi Goldenberg, and Elizabeth Dodson Gray. They too reject the hierarchy in traditional
religions and cry out for a more egalitarian world view. Feminist
theologians speak out against the male God in the sky and the
lingering Christian view that the world was created specifically for
man and that he has the right to use nature and women as he
pleases.[6] Nor is it surprising that the political philosophy in
feminist utopian fiction is most akin to anarchism, for women are
tired of being ruled, manipulated, and exploited by authoritarian
figures. So, too, is Bessie Head's protagonist.

Throughout Elizabeth's madness, there existed the possibility of being healed and made sane by working in a vegetable
garden with Kenosi. Kenosi had about her a quiet strength and
purposefulness that appealed to Elizabeth. As they worked together, "Elizabeth clung to the woman. There seemed to be no
other justification for her continued existence, so near to death was
she" (p. 89). She found in the uneducated, hardworking Kenosi a
"knowingness and grasp of life" that made her beautiful (p. 90).
Most important of all, Kenosi needs her. Kenosi tells her, "you
must never leave the garden ... I cannot work without you: (p. 142).
Her relationship with this woman keeps in sight the possibility of
something quite different from the patriarchal relationships she
has in the nightmare world: their "work-relationship has been
established on the solid respect of one partner for another" (p. 160).
Kenosi enables Elizabeth to maintain her belief that egalitarian
relationships are possible. Sello's comment to Elizabeth about her
relationship with Dan also helps to save her: "Elizabeth, love isn't
like that. Love is two people mutually feeding each other, not only
living on the soul of the other like a ghoul!" (p. 197).

Elizabeth withstands the cruelty and torture of Medusa and the two men who inhabit her madness through not giving in to their view of her as nothing. At one point she tells Sello that he is making a mistake, for she is God too (p. 38). Although they almost totally annihilate her sense of self, their misogynist behavior only serves to confirm her faith in the opposite of everything they represent. Throughout her struggle against these symbols of the patriarchal power system which people her hallucinations, she continues to articulate her faith in goodness, love, equality, and inner strength.

The movement toward mysticism found in feminist philosophy is obviously present in Elizabeth's as well. Elizabeth has been tested by the nightmare of madness created by Sello in his role as spritual mentor. Once she has passed through this hell, her knowledge of evil helps her to rediscover an impersonal, mystical love. She is transported into a state in which there are "no private hungers to be kissed, loved, adored. And yet there was a feeling of being kissed by everything; by the air, the soft flow of life, people's smiles and friendships." This "vast and universal love" equalizes all things and all people. Elizabeth emerges from her hell with a confirmed belief in such love and a "lofty serenity of soul nothing could shake" (p. 202). At the end of the book she recognizes that humankind's fundamental error is the "relegation of all things holy to some unseen Being in the sky. Since man was not holy to man, he could be tortured for his complexion, he could be misused, degraded and killed" (p. 205).

Bessie Head choses to focus on sexism rather than racism in *A Question of Power*. This forces her African readers, more familiar with racism, to see the similarities between the two and their common root in the philosophy of domination. Men degrade, manipulate, and abuse women in Elizabeth's nightmare, basically because they fail to perceive sacredness in them. Elizabeth advocates a philosophy that insists upon the sacredness of all life because of her subjection to this patriarchal behavior. This is typical of the evolution of feminist thought. That is why feminists speak of ecological and peace issues as well as equal rights; and that is why they speak of equal rights not only for women but also for the poor, the handicapped, and the racially oppressed.

Buchi Emecheta[7] and Bessie Head[8] speak for millions of Black African women through their novels, for they describe what it is like to be female in patriarchal African cultures. In *The Joys of Motherhood*, Nigerian Buchi Emecheta focuses upon the patriarchal beliefs and practices that must be eradicated—son preference, polygamy, double standards, rigid sex roles, and above all, the glorification of motherhood in order to render women powerless. In *A Question of Power*, set in Botswana, Bessie Head portrays even more abusive patriarchal behavior, relates it to all forms of oppression, and presents a philosophy for living quite differently.

The two novels describe the spiritual growth of their protagonists, Nnu Ego and Elizabeth. Both "female heroes" rise above their suffering by resisting the training for submission that they have had within the patriarchal culture. Both finally are able to release themselves from dependency because they have acknowledged at least inwardly the patriarchal cause of their suffering. Through very personal experiences, the two protagonists show us the social and spiritual consequences of a power structure based upon a philosophy of domination. Buchi Emecheta focuses upon the social and Bessie Head upon the spiritual consequences. As the protagonists explore these domains, they venture into feminist consciousness and thereby gain confidence in the rightness of their own vision.

Notes

[1] Adrienne Rich, *Of Woman Born: Motherhood as Experience and Institution* (New York: Bantam, 1977), p. 20.

[2] Buchi Emecheta, *The Joys of Motherhood*, African Writers Series, 227 (London: Heinemann, 1980), p. 9. All further references to this work appear in the text.

[3] Buchi Emecheta's other novels are *In the Ditch* (1973), *Second-Class Citizen* (1974), *The Bride Price* (1976), *The Slave Girl* (1977), *The Moonlight Bride* (1983), and *Double Yoke* (1982).

[4] Bessie Head has written two other novels *When Rain Clouds Gather* (1969) and *Maru* (1971). She has published a collection of short stories *The Collector of Treasures* (1977) and the history, as told by its people, of *Serowe: Village of the Rain Wind* (1981). She has also written plays for television, children's stories, articles, and peotry.

[5] Bessie Head, *A Question of Power*, African Writers Series, 149 (London: Heinemann, 1974), pp. 28, 144. All further references to this work appear in the text.

[6] See for example, Rosemary Ruether's *New Woman New Earth: Sexist Ideologies and Human Liberation* (New York: The

Seabury Press, 1975), Naomi Goldenberg's *Changing of the Gods: Feminism and the End of Traditional Religions* (Voaron: Vwxon Pewaa, 1979), and Elizabeth Dodson Gray's *Green Paradise Lost* (Wellesley, M.A.: Roundtable Press, 1981).

[7] For further information about Buchi Emecheta, see an interview with her in the September 1981 issue of *Opzij*, a Dutch feminist monthly and her autobiographical reflections, "Head Above Water," in *Kunapipi*, 3, No. 1 (1981), 81-90. The chapter about her in Lloyd W. Brown's *Women Writers in Black Africa* (Westport, CT: Greenwood Press, 1981) was written before the publication of her last three novels. See also "Buchi Emecheta," *Africa Woman*, No. 2 (Jan. 1976), 48 ff; Judith Wilson, "Buchi Emecheta: Africa from a Woman's View," *The Bride Price*," *World Literature Written in English*, 16 No. 2 (Nov. 1977), 310 ff; Alice Walker, "A Writer Because of, Not in Spite of Her Children," *Ms.*, 4 No. 7 (Jan. 1976), 40 ff; and Marie Umeh, "African Women in Transition in the Novels of Buchi Emecheta,: *Présence Africaine*, 116 (1980), 190-99.

[8] For further information about Bessie Head, see an interview with her in *Conversation with African Writers: Interviews with Twenty-six African Authors*, ed. Lee Nichols (Washington, D.C.: Voice of America, 1981), pp. 49-57 and her statement about her life which precedes her short story "Witchcraft" in *Ms.*, No. 5 (Nov. 1975), pp. 72-73. See also Charlotte Bruner, "Bessie Head: Restless in a Distant Land" in *When the Drumbeat Changes*, ed. Carolyn Parker et al. (Washington, D.C.: Three Continents, 1981), 261-77 and the chapter on her work in Lloyd W. Brown's *Women Writers in Black Africa*, pp. 158-79.

Power and the Question of Good and Evil in Bessie Head's Novels

Virginia Ola

> Maybe a dark shadow had been created to balance
> the situation. Maybe some blot of human wrong
> had to happen to force Maru to identify himself
> with the many wrongs of mankind.[1]

It is significant that the foregoing lines should appear in a passage which describes a garden of yellow daisies where a lover meditates on the boundless joys of a romantic relationship whose days of "torrential expressions of love" far outweigh the occasional malice and unhappiness which are always part of most human situations.

Maru, the protagonist of Besie Head's novel, *Maru*, is in love with nature, particularly the yellow daisies which dotted the surroundings of his little house on a hill, mainly because they "were the only flowers which resembled the face of his wife and the sun of his love" (p. 5). Despite this fairy-tale and magical environment the love in question is haunted by "a low line of black boiling clouds" which manifests itself in vicious malicious moods occasioned by the guilt of its violation of Margaret's first love which Maru, her husband, had executed without remorse. Maru's victory of necessity is therefore tainted by evil and its agony follows him all the days of his life.

This structure of the conflict of good and evil in human lives and society is central in Bessie Head's vision and controls the structural landscape and characterization in her three novels. Invariably it is engendered by the ruthless and unjust exercise of power.

This dichotomy attains its most frightening dimension in *A Question of Power* from which readers emerge unable to establish any connection between the harrowing experience recorded therein and the beautiful pastoral scenes which straddle those scenes. Behind all these are the nightmarish accounts of intrigue, hatred, callousness and intense mental torture which the main character is subjected to. Commenting on this aspect of her works, Head herself says:

> Such peaceful rural scenes would be hastily snatched to form the backdrop to tortuous novels. Perceptive fans sensed the disparity, the disparity between the peaceful simplicity of village life and a personality more complex than village life could ever be. They would say: "I like the bits about Botswana life but I found your second/third novel difficult to read ...."[2]

The above statement defines succinctly the dominant structural design of Head's novels, which she herself has called "tortuous." It was in the attempt to come to grips with that same overpowering quality, especially in *A Question of Power*, that Arthur Ravenscroft wrote:

> It seems to me that with Bessie Head ... each novel both strikes out anew, and also reshoulders the same burden. It is as if one were observing a process that involves simultaneously progression, introgression, and circumgression; but also (and here I believe lies her particular creative power) organic growth in both her art and her central concerns. For all our being lured as readers into the labyrinth of Elizabeth's tortured mind in *A Question of Power*, and then, as it were, left there to face with her the phantasmagoric riot of nightmare and horror, one nevertheless senses throughout that the imagination which unleashes this fevered torrent resides in a creative mind that is exceedingly tough[3]

This toughness accounts for the special bleakness which we find in her moral vision and world view, despite their constant celebration of rural harmony, innocence, love and solidarity; qualities vital for the creation of the "new worlds" which Head advocates ceaselessly in these novels. It also shows that in that moral quest she never loses sight of the harsh realities, such as racism, sexism, poverty and sometimes fear, which threaten the full realization of that dream. The cooperative in *When Rain Clouds Gather* is such a new world, at least its possibility, which the characters attempt to create from the harsh and dry landscape of rural Botswana, and from the broken pieces of their past. Head's vision is dominated by visionaries, the creators of these new worlds, and the demons which constantly thwart their efforts, through political or sexual power. In her words Head herself has admitted that her earlier work was filled with "personal data and responses to challenges that were on the whole internal and private."[4] The different stages of that life are recreated in her three novels mostly through the experiences of characters whose problems articulate Head's own moral vision and fear of power.

This vision includes a keen search for human, social, sexual and political values within a harmonious social order. Understandably the limitations of women's roles, their disadvantages and their bruised self-image feature prominently in her novels. The black and coloured of South Africa, women and all the politically oppressed, are victims of the power she dreads so much. *When Rain Clouds Gather*, her first novel, deals with the search for roots from different perspectives, and as it affects characters of different social backgrounds, all victims of political, tribal, sexual or even religious power. The book reminds the reader of the drought-stricken world of Ngugi wa Thiongo's *Petals of Blood* where characters with different visions and problems bond together in search of political justice and spiritual regeneration. Makhaya is such a character.

He is a typical victim of a political power that manifests itself in racial oppression, a situation which Head knows by personal experience. As a young Zulu, he fled into Botswana like Head herself, to escape prosecution for anti-apartheid activities in South Africa. In the small village of Golema Mmidi he finds a group of refugees who, like himself, have suffered, endured great griefs and bitterness, and are trying to make new ordered lives for themselves through cooperative effort in an agricultural project lead by Gilbert Balfour, a young British agronomist, who likewise dreads the comfort of his emotionally arid middle-class background. Even old Dinorego and Mma Millipede have earlier in life suffered as victims of power abuse. Makhaya finally grows out of the hate which was gradually consuming his being. In Ravenscroft's words:

> Against a political background of self-indulgent,
> self-owning traditional chiefs and self-seeking,
> new politicians more interested in power than
> people, the village of Golema Mmidi is offered as

a difficult alternative: not so much a rural utopia for the Africa of the future to aim at, as a means of personal and economic independence and inter- dependence, where the qualities that count are benign austerity, reverence for the lives of ordi- nary people (whether university-educated experts or illiterate villagers), and, above all, the ability to break out of the prison of selfhood without de- stroying individual privacy and integrity.[5]

Head's idealism therefore takes full cognizance of the brutal realism of the world in which it is meant to be realized. It is posed against such obstacles as the long-standing conservatism of the local people and their suspicion of new techniques; a reactionary chief who is jealous of the cooperative's encroachment on his traditional privileges, especially that of cattle speculation. Even in this environment, the personal fears of the participants, their insecurities and the natural urge to dominate others also have to be fought, for these factors are the evil which constantly threatens the success of this creative endeavour. The issues are those of power and identity, and the energy and commitment with which Makhaya plunges into the venture soon purge him of the disillusionment and self-destructive hatred with which he first enters the new community. His eventual union with Paulina Sobeso, a passionate and lonely woman who is also fleeing a disastrous marriage in northern Botswana, symbolizes this newly found harmony. How- ever the venture transcends just personal love and harmony for it also symbolizes harmony between characters of different races, different sexes and different ages, as well as the victory of love over oppressive power. Brown describes it as "a healing moral growth, reflecting not only the creative purposefulness of individual members but also an unusual degree of harmony between the races and the sexes."[6] Commenting further on Head's moral vision Brown continues:

...her moral idealism remains the most powerfully effective and most distinguishing feature of her three novels.... Her idealism nurtures her strength as a realistic novelist, enabling her to turn uproot- edness into a vantage point from which she scru- tinizes social institutions as they usually are—as they distort individual personality through power- oriented definitions of race, sex, religion and indi- vidualism.[7]

Head's vision also searches out for complementarity of identities. This complementarity functions either as the necessity for an individual to realize his full potential by recognizing his own strengths and weaknesses, and thereby seeking to identify with another character who possesses what he himself lacks; it also features as two characters functioning as the positive and negative qualities of one person, much in the manner of Dr. Jekyll and Mr. Hyde. Her first novel operates on the first level, while the second type is dramatized in her second and third novels. Makhaya and Gilbert discover this essential unity in their first long conversation; that while Gilbert is running "away" from England, Makhaya is running "into" a settled life with wife and children. "He wanted a few simple answers on how to live well and sanely. He wanted to undo the complexity of hatred and humiliation that had dominated his life for so long." His life had been a battleground for inner conflicts and strifes, and the opportunities at Golema Mmidi gave him the opportunity to put together its fragmented pieces. His sensitivity, trustworthiness, patience and a fascinating ability to make people do his bidding without exerting too much energy are the qualities so clearly lacking in Gilbert, the rational scientist:

> Gilbert was a complete contrast to this wavering, ambiguous world in which Makhaya lived. He was first and foremost a practical down-to-earth kind of man, intent only on being of useful service to his fellow men. There was nothing fanciful in him, yet the workings of his mind often confused and fascinated Makhaya. It was like one gigantic storage house of facts and figures and plans and intuitive impressions. (WRCG. p. 81).

Makhaya appreciates the contrast and decides to adopt an attitude of compromise, considering Gilbert's company and friendship more important than differences in character makeup. From Gilbert, Dinorego, Mma Millipede he imbibes much of human philosophy—the values of generosity, sharing, companionship, foregiveness and positiveness; and finally, "Loving one woman had brought him to this realization: that it was only people who could bring the real rewards of living; that it was only people who give love and happiness" (p. 163). Makhaya's transformation is important to Bessie Head because it once more underscores her belief that the ravages of power can be destroyed if the good in man prevails over the evil in him and if love is posited in place of power.

Besides Matenge and other selfish traditional rulers, and such stooges like Joas Tsepe, this destructive element is symbolically represented by the harsh wasteland of Botswana, and by the arresting images of death and decay which Head has given cosmic significance. They all underscore the harsh moral landscape of the novel created by the brutal power of Matenge. The barbed wire fence which Makhaya successfully crosses over signifies his victory over all the malignant forces ranged against him and all the visionaries in the novel. The combined force of their personal inner powers triumphs over all the obstacles and gives birth to a new social order and new personal values for all the participants. The rebirth is total, and demonstrates the power of creativity over evil; a fact which the beautiful artistic productions of Sobeso's son even while in the grips of drought and consumption amply demonstrate.

Maru, Head's second novel, again integrates the political and the personal in its exploration of the author's vision vis-a-vis power, social and psychological. Maru, the main character, like Makhaya, forsakes the life of fame and importance for love and peace of mind. Head is fascinated by the mystery of human life and the inner strengths buried in the lives of characters like Maru. Brown noticed this fascination when he wrote: "The inner power fascinates Head on another basis. It is intensely individual and private, but at the same time it is the absolute prerequisite in the human form, for the achievement of public harmony based on social justice."[8]

Maru is Head's second novel and its complex emotional structure has been commented on in the introductory pages of this essay. In line with the first novel it handles the issues of power and love, now enacted with all the storm and stress that accompany them. It is part of Head's well-known psychological insight that the social and emotional upheaval of this drama are set in motion by Margaret Cadmore, a woman without identity, an outcast in a hostile society whose inner strength, goodness and resilience are pitted against the political power of two totems, born into royalty, feared, respected and pampered.

Both Maru and Moleka not only fall in love with Margaret but undergo drastic character transformation. Maru observed that this powerless woman was the only person in the community who looked him directly in the face. In Moleka's case Maru noticed that "the savage arrogant Moleka was no longer there, but some other person like himself—humbled and defeated before all the beauty of the world" (p. 57).

Margaret's internal power derives from her upbringing by her British foster parent from whom she receives a fully strengthened personality which in the great trials and tribulations of her life guarantee the continuance of her inner wholeness and enable her to survive "both heaven and hell." In this situation Margaret feels warmth, love and freedom but with Pete, Seth and Morafi the garish and revolting caricatures and clowns who represent the school at Dilepe to which Margaret was deployed as a teacher the haunting reality of evil is introduced into the heroine's joy. They constitute the full embodiments of the impersonal and brutal social milieu in which Margaret confronts daily insults from the young and the old; by looks, words and actions. Hers is a life lived between the contest of good and evil, each working by its own form of power.

But the play of power in the context of good and evil is even more subtly explored in the deadly struggle between Maru and Moleka for the love of Margaret. Here lies the central drama of the book whose paradox lies in the fact that the passive heroine indirectly engineers this conflict between two powerful totems just by being herself. Significantly she is not offered a choice and never fully realises the depth of the revenge which she awoke in Maru. As always she takes recourse in her stoicism which had helped her to endure the barbarism and sadism of the society she lives in. It was a feeling of being "permanently unwanted by society." In Maru's hands however she finds herself in company of a visionary and a demon.

Maru can be seen as the representative individual experimenting on the possibilities of the limitless power which he possesses by virtue of being the hereditary paramount chief - elect of the Botswana, waiting to be installed after his predecessor's death; but rather than exploit the political and social privileges of that position he surprises and shocks the community of Dilepe by giving up these gains in favour of an amorous relationship with an outcast. This choice brings him into collision with Moleka who was Margaret's first love. But Moleka has been his best friend before now, and Head plays their essential oneness throughout the book. In character they both possess contradictory traits, positive and negative; each crystallizing in description and action the totality of the personality of the other friend. In fact Ravenscroft goes as far as to ask: "And, are we sure, at the end, that the two chief male characters, Maru and Moleka, who are close intimate friends until they become bitter antagonists, are indeed two separate fictional characters, or that they are symbolic extensions of contending character-traits within the same man?"[9] The new Moleka, who falls in love with Margaret, has more of Maru than of the old Moleka who is arrogant and brutal, but the scheming insensitive Maru is more like the brazen Moleka than the old sensitive Maru, "who had all the stuff that ancient kings and chiefs were made of," the Maru who carries his gods within him (p. 36). He is as unfathomable as Moleka is predictable, yet remains the only one who realizes that it is Moleka's kingdom that was unfathomable:

> It was only Maru who saw their relationship in its true light. They were kings of opposing king-doms. It was Moleka's kingdom which was unfathomable, as though shut behind a heavy iron door. There had been no such door for Maru. He dwelt everywhere. He'd mix the prosaic of every-day life with the sudden beauty of a shooting star ... Moleka was the only person who was his equal. They alone loved each other, but they were opposed because they were kings (*Maru*, p. 34).

In nothing were their differences of character highlighted as in their attitude to women. Moleka has built himself a most unenviable reputation as an insensitive and sexually exploitative young man. As a result his mother is condemned to spend her life caring for his host of girlfriends and their illegitimate children. In Head's words "Moleka and women were like a volcanic explosion in a dark tunnel. Moleka was the only one to emerge, on each occasion, unhurt, smiling" (p. 35) With Maru it was totally different:

> Maru fell in love with his women. He'd choose them with great care and patience. There was always some outstanding quality; a special ten-derness in the smile, a beautiful voice or some-thing in the eyes which suggested mystery and hidden dreams. He associated these with the beauty in his own heart, only to find that a tender smile and a scheming mind went hand in hand, a beautiful voice turned into a dominat-ing viper who confused the inner Maru, who was king of heaven, with the outer Maru and his earthly position of future paramount chief of a tribe (*Maru*, p. 35)

It is therefore not surprising that with such heightened sensitivity Maru often took ill after the failure of his love affairs. But Head treats this dichotomy with her usual irony; Maru's methods are cold, calculating and ruthless, the normal methods of those who wield destructive power, the same type he has dissociated himself from by renouncing his chieftaincy and all its political implications. Such an act is in direct opposition to his use of his three spies who sniff, inform and "fix" Maru's plans to tear away Moleka from Margaret. Despite such unorthodox methods of dealing with his rival Head insists that Maru acts according to the directions of the gods he carries within him. It is, after all, another way of exercising power. There is perhaps some logic to Maru's winning of Margaret. The latter possesses that quality of mystery which is part of Maru's make-up, as well as that mine of inner strength and individuality which is her legacy from her British foster-mother, Margaret Cadmore. Bessie Head is exploring a state of moral ambiguity in which most human beings have a bit of the visionary and the demon in them, a balance of good and evil. Maru the schemer is not very different from Moleka, the arch manipulator; and Moleka who loves Margaret is not very different from the Maru who walks with gods and goddesses. Margaret symbolizes, in her retention of her love for Moleka, even after her marriage to Maru, Head's ideal woman confronting the issue of male protectiveness, possession on one hand, and male crude power on the other, by a firm sense of choices, which amounts to a demonstration of her own inner power. In other words she is Maru's equal, and as an artist has dreamt Maru's dreams as Maru discovers later to his dismay and joy. Head does not resolve this delicate issue in the course of the story, for despite Maru's overt victory over Moleka his new, almost idyllic life with Margaret has permanently been tainted by a black, boiling cloud, typified by moments of brooding, jealousy and malicious meditation when he wonders whether it was a superior kind of love or a superior kind of power that Moleka had. Whichever one it was he remains lord over the other room in his wife's heart. This presence undermines the degree of his victory, and serves as a constant reminder to him of that dangerous aspect of his personality, the use of ruthless power for selfish reasons which is the true demon that thwarts the effort of visionaries like himself to build a more humane society.

In *A Question of Power*, Head's power-hungry demon is recreated in the character of Dan. This novel is also her most complex, most ambitious and most profoundly frightening in what it says about the reality of power, loneliness, exile and ultimately insanity. In Ravenscroft's words:

> One wonders again and again whether the phantom world that comes to life whenever Elizabeth is alone in her hut could have been invented by a novelist who had not herself gone through similar experiences, so frighteningly and authentically does it all pass before one's eyes. But there is no confusion of identity between the novelist and the character, and Bessie Head makes one realize often how close is the similarity between the fevered creations of a deranged mind and the insanities of deranged societies.[10]

The novel is set in Motabeng and the events are filtered through the disturbed consciousness of Elizabeth, the central character, who in the process of the story undergoes a period of acute inner distress with repetitive cycles of nervous breakdown from which she recovers weaker and more frightened about the world around her. Her hallucinations, fear and obsessive self-doubts are symptoms of her insecurities as a woman and as an outsider in the society. The social discrimination which Margaret suffered among the Botswana in *Maru* reaches harrowing proportions in Elizabeth's nightmares in *A Question of Power*, where one of her tormentors never ceases to remind her that she is "a coloured woman." In addition she is frightened of the possibility of running mad like her mother who died in a mental institution where she was locked up for her indiscretion in having a baby for the black stable boy. The principal of her mission school revealed the secret to her when she was thirteen and his prophecy almost came true.

In the unfolding of her solitary mental drama Elizabeth's nightmares are dominated by two characters, Sello and Dan, of whom the former lives in the village of Motabeng, though she does not know him personally. Sello was a crop farmer and cattle breeder. These two characters turn the protagonist's mind into a battleground as they compete for the domination and possession of her personality. Sello is the symbol of love and compassion, elevated to the role of a god or goddess, and who for four years has been "a ghostly, persistent commentator on all her thoughts, perceptions and experiences .... First, he had introduced his own soul, so softly like a heaven of completeness and perfection: (p. 14). Sello symbolically appears as a man-like apparition or hallucination sitting in Elizabeth's room at night, constantly revealing to her spriritual truths; "Love isn't like that. Love is two people mutually feeding each other" (p. 14). Commenting on Sello's personality the author writes:

> It seemed almost incidental that he was African. So vast had his inner perceptions grown over the years that he preferred an identification with mankind to an identification with a particular environment. And yet as an African, he seemed to have made one of the most perfect statements: "I am just anyone ..." It wasn't as though his society were not evil too, but nowhere else could he have acquired the kind of humility which made him feel, within, totally unimportant, totally free from his own personal poisons—pride and arrogance and egoism of the soul. It had always been like this, for him—a hunger after the things of the soul in which other preoccupations were submerged; they were intuitions mostly of what is right ....[11]

In his God-like humility Sello has also transcended the bleak arid barrenness of the soul which Elizabeth knew so well. He loved not only each particle of earth around him, but also the natural events of sunrise, including the people and animals of Motabeng. It was a love which included the whole universe. Sello had said to himself one evening, "I might have died before I found this freedom of heart." To Head, "That was another perfect statement, to him—love was freedom of heart" (p. 11). Sello therefore stands for perfection, for the God-like in man. In this he is a later development of Maru, and by inference one of Head's visionaries and a symbol of the good, but he also stands for evil in a very subtle way.

Dan on the other hand epitomizes destructive male egoism and all that is vile, personally debasing and obscene. The resultant wild display of wreckage and power in the form of unbridled eroticism and sexuality constitutes the greatest threat to Elizabeth's weakened mental health and demonstrates Head's apprehension of evil and its organic relationship to power. The heroine's greatest source of torture arises from Dan's ability to violate her mind with his practised, depraved obscenities. He flaunts before her what Ravenscroft call "his gargantuan sexual exploits with an incredible succession of sexually insatiable females ..."[12] Their names: Madam Loose-Bottom, Body Beautiful, Squelch Squelch,

Sugar-Plum, The Womb, Miss Pink Sugar-Icing and Miss Pelican-Beak, to name a few of the seventy-one, are telling enough. Dan's beastliness and exploitative sexuality remind the reader of Moleka's sexual abandon and bigotry, and what Head calls "the African man's loose carefree sexuality which lacks "the stopgaps of love and tenderness and personal romantic treasuring of women" (p. 137). It is to her a frightening aspect of male domination and abuse of power which by extension manifest themselves in the oppression of the weak, the lonely and outcasts in most societies of the world. Dan is literally a tyrant, and he understood the mechanics of power like Hitler and Napoleon. In his hands, she lives over and over again the torments of mankind's past and present history. To explore the reality of this power-machine in human history Head takes a comprehensive imaginative sweep through world religions, cultures, and myths from Osiris, Medusa, Buddha and even Christ. Through all these Head explores the operations of evil in human affairs, for the question of good and evil is an over-riding concern in this work.

Elizabeth's torments also provide Head with an opportunity to once more explore the warring of good and evil in the same individual. The Sello/Dan polarity is a more frightening development of the Maru/Moleka unity in dichotomy theme, and a negation of the Makhaya/Gilbert compromise. It is a polarity which Head never really resolves but rather awakens her readers' awareness of its existence, and points to ways of confronting it. The fact that the God-like Sello has the vicious and vile Medusa of Greek mythology as his alter ego, and that Dan after all, is just an extension of Medusa, underscores the complexity of this reality of the battle between good and evil in the world, and in us. Ironically too, Sello as God remains ambivalent, passive and sometimes overwhelmed by the evil that is his own creation and a function of himself. Sello had created the Dan image to test Elizabeth, as the former informs her after the defeat of Dan. Elizabeth realizes this, or at least suspects this treachery earlier on:

> She could not sort out Sello, the shuttling movements he made between good and evil, the way he had introduced absolute perfection and flung muck in her face. ... His other voice, so quietly, insistently truthful, barely rose above the high storm of obscenity. The two voices often seemed to merge (p. 137).

He had been responsible for creating the demons which peopled her nights and threatened to dominate her days too, turning her whole existence into a howling inferno. Yet she felt some affection for the real man, as well as some hatred. He has seen that evil and good travel side by side in the same personality" (p. 98). Elizabeth eventually sees this too, and this recognition heralds her recovery and self-growth, "and from the degradation and destruction of her life had arisen a still, lofty serenity of soul nothing could shake" (p. 202). Amidst all her torments and the sexual cesspit which ravaged her soul the only sane centre of purposeful, expanding and hopeful activity in this desolation was the Motabeng Secondary school where she taught, and the agricultural cooperative effort under Eugene, the shining example of men who have opposed death, evil and greed, and have surrounded themselves with a "creative ferment." These periods offer periodic breaks in her life, which can be described as that of "a person driven out of her own house while demons rampaged within, turning everything upside down" (p. 49). Her recovery is a testament of the ability of the human will to overcome evil after the soul's journey through hell and purgatory.

Bessie Head's three novels demonstrate the unleashing of a powerful imagination, willing to explore the inner recesses of the human personality to explore the significance of power of all forms in its make-up, and to map out the constant warring of the powerful forces of good and evil in each individual. This ambitious philosophical investigation is finally channelled towards the plight of the alienated and helpless individual in society, particularly his plight as an exile from an oppressive regime like that of South Africa. The hope is for a more humane society which she hopes can be achieved only by each individual confronting the horrors of history, as well as the horrors within himself, so that the demons of brute and naked power, cruelty and oppression may not wreck the work of visionaries engaged in the realization of this humane society.

Notes:

[1] Bessie Head, *Maru* (London: Heinemann, 1971), p. 8. Further references to this text can be found within the essay.

[2] Bessie Head, Biographical Notes: "A Search of Historical Continuity and Roots". A Short Paper presented by the author at the Annual International Conference of African Literature held at the University of Calabar, Nigeria, February 1982.

[3] Arthur Ravenscroft: "The Novels of Bessie Head" in *Aspects of South African Literature* (ed.) Christopher Heywood (London, Ibadan, Nairobi, Lusaka: Heinemann, 1976), p. 175.

[4] Ibid., p. 5.

[5] Ravenscroft. "The Novels of Bessie Head", p. 177.

[6] Lloyd Brown, *Women Writers in Black Africa* (West Port: Greenwood Press, 1981), p. 164

[7] Ibid. , p. 160.

[8] Bessie Head *When Rain Clouds Gather*, London: Heinemann Educational Books, 1972), p. 11: Further references to this text will be inserted within the essay.

[9] Brown, op. cit. p. 168.

[10] Ravenscroft, op. cit. p. 179.

[11] Ibid., p. 184.

[12] Ibid., p. 184.

The World of
Bessie Head

Ella Robinson

In Botswana, her country of exile from South Africa, Bessie Head sat down to pen *Maru, A Question of Power, The Collector of Treasures* and *Serowe: Village of the Rain Winds*, partly as protest, but largely as portrayal of her philosophy. Head's allegiance to substance is based on a sound belief that sanity is possible even when attacked by the insanity of presumed superiority as a result of skin color and hair texture. In South Africa, as Head portrays it, sanity is a state sometimes won and then lost, but always it is to be pursued. The fight is for a humane society; the battle is personal, psychological, emotionally stressful. Head rejects a prose of nihilism in this war and presents a healthy correlative undergirded by strong spiritual convictions. In Head's works there is no pristine idea of existence; everything is seasoned by analysis or by comparative revelation.

Thus in *Maru* Margaret and Maru's dreams suggest that they have something in common (p. 10). Maru's dreams and visions are systematic of the creative mind. What he wants is to rid his own mind of tribal cruelty. And in this process his objective is to build a new world (p. 108). To come to this position, he speaks to his gods who tell him to "do things outside any narrow enclosure of social order" (p. 109). His profound belief in the saving grace of visions is seen in what he teaches. His friend Moleka develops a visionary eye through Maru's tutelage. These facts are noble, yet Maru, as we all sometimes do, knew his moments of despair. He knew how to use arrogance and force, though deep within he was kind and humble. Arrogance was a more outward shield; force was used to carry out the dictates of his gods.

Head's protagonist, Maru, must show strength for he hates weak self-pity. His overriding hunger is for love. When we meet him he has already the spiritual prerequisites. He is a leader of men and a lover of flowers, yellow daisies to be exact. Moreover, he has insight and poetry. Head tells us:

> He'd mix the prosaic of everyday life with the
> beauty of a shooting star. Folks who had nothing
> never turned into your queens and goddesses
> (p. 34).

Maru is shown as having kingly qualities, he is a chief in the old style. He knows how to use rhetoric to his advantage. Through his sister, he creates in Dekelede the artist par excellence. She paints and paints, and paints just for him, to satisfy his cravings. In developing herself, she serves as an outstanding symbol for her people. She shows the snobbish that in fact Bushmen can rise to a great pinacle.

Maru's and Dikelede's love has something to do with justice, but the magic is greater than love, law, justice. Head speaks neither of absolute justice nor of absolute truth. Instead the stress lies with voices, the gods, and the forces that inspire all of nature.

These forces are quite apparent in *A Question of Power*. The overriding image where these factors are at work is Hell! Personalities breed a state where balances of power are necessary. The "loosely-knit personality" can easily be preyed upon by dominant powerful personalities. Insecurities are like blood in shark-infested waters. The object of *A Question of Power* is to examine inner and outer forces. The omniscient narrator explains.

> There seems to be a mutual agreement in the beginning that an examination of inner hells was meant to end all hells forever (p.   12).

And in hell, love is hard to come by. It is distorted. The source is Elizabeth's immediate ancestry: a white mother, a black man who was stable boy as father. Then there is the insanity of the mother, the act of being yanked from her natural mother and the cruelty of her teachers who retell this story so that she will vividly remember her "proper" place. On top of this Elizabeth marries, no doubt, still longing for love and learns that her husband is a philanderer who sleeps with men and women. She is thus left with a son, without a husband or any other close family members. This is, of course, a tragedy.

And then constantly there rests in the back of Elizabeth's mind the fact that her skin is less black than "real" Africans, and her hair less kinky. She, therefore, assumes she is less interesting sexually. Elizabeth's tribulations cause her to seek perfection in absolute good. She combines her psyche with both male and female qualities, brings these qualities which we all possess to the forefront and is possessed by them. She then turns to the human family to access its combinations: the Asian, the white, the black, the brown. She comes to see evil as eternal and as an integral part of being in the current of life where one raises the current of his maturing self to a higher level. But one pays dearly for this growth.

While living with an Asian family she learns the concepts of Buddhism. This knowledge "clothes" her every choice during the major portion of the novel. And clothing becomes terribly important to her. The phrase that let us know this is "vesture garments." And so image in *A Question of Power* is persuasive. It speaks for and to the inner soul. Outer responses reinforce or detract from the soul's growth. What we speak of here is suffering, a necessary experience to elevate the soul.

The omniscient narrator sheds a light into Elizabeth's mind, a mind struggling toward Nirvana. "It seemed to her as though all suffering gave people and nations a powerful voice for the future and a common meeting ground, because the types of people in *A Question of Power* that Sello refers to as "the Gods" turned out on observation to be ordinary, practical, sane people, seemingly their only distinction being that they had consciously concentrated on spiritual earnings" (p. 31). No group of people can claim superiority to another, for the individual may appear and reappear in many different groups of the human family. One is most blessed when he does not have to reappear as human at all.

This belief causes Elizabeth to see the beauty in evolution and to equate it with perfection and love. This vision, however, gives Elizabeth neither strength nor peace. She is more and more possessed by her male counterpart, Sello. Sello explains to Elizabeth that "God in its absolute all-powerful form is a disaster to its holder" (pp. 35-6). To see all is to be tempted to do evil. And the more one knows, the less secure one is.

Elizabeth takes this notion to an extreme. She allows her insecurities to create fear. In the midst of it rises paranoia and self doubt. Those with skin of a darker hue come to despise her. She takes on the sin of her white ancestry. Nevertheless, "her soul is a black shapeless mass with wings." She envies the poverty-stricken masses who seem to have reached nirvana in their ability to cope with daily life in peace and security. And here she is an obvious part of all mankind writhing in confusion, insane then again sane. One of Elizabeth's major problems is that she knows she is a part of God, and to know this shakes the material foundations of the soul.

Good and evil, catastrophe and triumph pervade Elizabeth's consciousness. She likes the African notion of evolution
"where none is high and none is low but all are equal" (p.   63).
Indeed, the most outstanding statement in the entire novel supports this concept of evolution. It reads:

> Be ordinary. Any assumption of greatness leads
> to a dog-eat-dog fight and incurs massive suffer-
> ing (p.   39).

Head believes that an important lesson Africa can teach the world
is indeed to be "ordinary". And so, the part of Elizabeth that is Sello
prefers an identification with mankind, rather than a particular
location or environment. Sello is more carefree than Elizabeth.
Thus her serious suffering side needs him. Like her, he has "a
hunger after the things of the soul, in which other preoccupations
were submerged ... so strong this time that a quiet and permanent
job filled his heart .... Everything felt right with him .... He loved
each particle of earth around him, the everyday event of sunrise,
the people and animals of the village of Motabeng; perhaps his love
included the whole universe.... Love was freedom of the heart"
(p.   11).

The character Dan in *A Question of Power* desires hate as
strongly as Sello wants love. In fact, Dan hates Elizabeth. He thinks
he is God. He is Sello's father. He breathes into a clay model the
breath of life; it stands and walks for Elizabeth. He then blasts
Elizabeth to a height even greater than Buddha. He takes her to
heaven where a river runs: this is the river of life, of returning and
maturing souls. This is the eternal river of love symbolized by
branches of grapes intertwined as a loving couple might embrace.

And so we see that the hate Dan Molomo knows is really a
part of love, for he is part of Sello and both men are parts of
Elizabeth. There is complexity, then, that is worth noting in Dan's
character. He has a fantastic craving for sensations and things are
"wonderful" to him—you name it, birth, death, sex, gestures or
facial features. What is more negative in Dan's personality is his
selfishness which reveals itself in his love of blood and baser
human instincts. Dan wants Sello dead.

In spite of Dan's demented notions, Elizabeth's and thus
Sello's direction is toward the equality of men.

From the beginning, Elizabeth has no distinct personality
apart from Sello. She is told by poverty-stricken apparitions that
she and Sello must strip themselves of "vesture garments". They

too much participate in poverty. This pronouncement seems innocent enough, but Elizabeth too, learns that she has killed in another life. We kill when we refuse to eliminate pain and poverty. And tears do not have the capacity to wash away this sin.

Elizabeth turns to prayer for an answer. She feels that her people are standing on the apron of a new world and prays, "Oh God .... May I never contribute to creating dead worlds, only new worlds" (p. 100). Now, as Elizabeth prays this prayer, she is talking to a part of herself, for she sees Sello as godlike. We are told "types like Sello were always Brahmins or Rama". Nevertheless, they are not perfect and are mere souls, energies, planets, universes, and all kinds of magic and mysteries. Elizabeth often reminds herself that the title God is a disaster. All seeing eyes are a madness (pp. 36-7). Anyone with a modicum of power just might become Lucifer.

In *Village of the Rain Wind* Head again discusses spiritual concepts as she explains how relatively easily missionaries were able to convert many in the village to Christianity. This was the case largely because the people had always prayed to spirits. And praying to God is, of course, praying to a spirit.

Head, as author, separates herself from the simple, loving attitude of those in her village. The complexity of her concept of love and spiritual qualities are found in "A Poem to Serowe". This poem succinctly presents the beauty of image in *Village of the Rain Wind*.

Epilogue—A Poem to Serowe

These I have loved:

The hours I spent collecting together my birds, my pathways, my sunsets, and shared them, with everyone; The small boys of this village and their homemade wire cars; The windy nights, when the vast land mass outside my door simulate the dark roar of the ocean.

—And those mysteries: that one bird call at dawn— that single solitary outdoor fireplace far in the bush that always captivates my eye .... The very old women of the village who know so well how to plow with a hoe; their friendly motherliness and insistent greetings as they pass my fence with

loads of firewood or water buckets on their heads;
My home at night and the hours I spend outside it
watching the yellow glow of the candle-light
through the curtains; The hours I spent inside it in
long, solitary thought.

These small joys were all I had, with nothing
beyond them, they were indulged in over and
over again, like my favorite books .... (p.   179)

The world of thought and of books is Head's world. The
earth and growing things made this world for her more livable. In
fact, people become an integral part of their surroundings in
Serowe: Village of the Rain Wind. When nature refused to cooperate
or a river dried up, the people moved on to build new villages. The
history and destiny of a people, then, is never divorced from
tradition and religious beliefs.

But while *Village of the Rain Wind* is largely factual, the
Collector of Treasures is fictionalized. The thirteen stories deal with
myths, witchcraft, migration, Christianity and love. In the story
entitled, "The Deep River: A Story of Ancient Tribal Migration,"
Christianity comes to disrupt traditional authority vested in the
chief. The notion of a loving God or Jesus is questioned in "Heaven
is not Closed," for how can a people support slavery, on the one
hand, and equality in God, on the other. This was the message of
the missionaries. In "Witchcraft" visions and voices merge with
jealousy. The use of witchcraft is shown as destructive. Head
suggests that inner resources should be collected and treasured. To
live "a poem of tenderness" one shows respect, love and kindness
to himself and his family and one lives to protect life and its sacred
qualities.

Head's challenge, thus, is anti-apartheid, anti-colonialism in
which can be implied anti-capitalism in its exploitative structure.
Her pronouncement is to be ordinary, not Marxist, though she
could clearly see the relationship between racism and capitalism.
What Head attacks head-on, however, are not monetary structures
but corrupt spiritual devotions. She fervently believed Africans
could be the ones to create a new world, a more just system. But the
journey of the soul should never be impeded in the process, for the
ideal state is to be found neither in art, justice nor money. It does
not exist on earth.

Of Human Trials and Triumphs

Femi Ojo-Ade

It costs a woman too much to love a man[1]

There are good women and good men but they seldom join their lives together. It's always this mess and foolishness.[2]

The children of a real woman do not get lean or die.[3]

Introduction: Bessie Head's Short Stories and the Oral Tradition

Critics have written at length on the late Bessie Head's novels, but not nearly enough attention has been paid to her short stories.[4] The neglect is, of course, symptomatic of the negative notion on the latter genre generally held by many a reader, as well as publishers. However, a study of Head's stories reveals that they are — to adapt her title — a collection of treasures complementary to the novels in content, contemporaneity and commitment to Head's life-long cause in the name of the common beings of her community.

Indeed, her use of that neglected art-form is more adequate than the novel in expressing the immediacy of the problems, the depth of the dilemma engulfing a whole people, the particular trauma of the writer's existence and, most importantly, her humanism in spite of it all. First, Africa's oral tradition, with its singular oneness with nature and its emphasis on the existence of that much mentioned but much maligned majority, has been excellently used by Bessie Head: the image that sticks to one's mind is that of the grand old man, Modise, sitting at the fireside surrounded by the youths of the village, relating stories of existential significance to the villagers. Just as our ancestors, the old man symbolizes a world of wisdom contemplative and critical of our pauperized present.

The youths are eager to learn lessons, while enjoying the stylistic dexterity of the storyteller (see *The Collector of Treasures*, p. 11). Furthermore, those stories relating events of "long ago," "once upon a time," underscore the communality of the people even in the face of travails that, interestingly enough, have remained a part of today's tragedy.

Bessie Head has successfully honed the qualities of that traditional art with the earnestness and verisimilitude of the European counterpart, thereby establishing a sense of authentic harmony with reader's experience. In essence, the Headian story merits the definition of the genre given by the critic, Robert Gorham Davis:

> A short story makes what began as a unique experience meaningful and communicable by relating it to other experiences, by placing it in the broad context of life, by shorwing what kind of experience it is.[5]

Her characters are at once individuals and types and, through them, Head observes life with the double vision of the common being and the community. The style, simple and down-to-earth, finds its characters with ease: the down-trodden, the desolate, the defeated, all non-heroic due to their estate but heroic as the centre of concern of the writer and, in several cases, as courageous commoners. The titles of the stories underscore that commonness, with the most appropriate being, "Life" (*The Collector* ..., p. 37). Bessie Head's well known biography of exile and its attendant socio-mental agony and alienation, of illegitimacy and its psychological torture translated into an existence of limbo, already gives an insight to the autobiographical context of the stories. The names of the characters tell a tale: *Gaenametse* (there-is-no-water) and *Dikeledi* (tears) are symbols of particular sufferings expressive of the existence of a whole people.

> Long ago, when the land was only cattle tracks and footpaths, the people lived together like a deep river. In this deep river which was unruffled by conflict or a movement forward, the people lived without faces, except for their chief, whose face was the face of all the people. (p. 1)

The chief was the people's face, but only in times of peace. In times of turmoil, individual faces surfaced, as it were, as a necessary process of the restoration of peace to the land. The stories pinpoint such unusual times, describing the pathos of communal life and the daily struggle for survival of a village immune, to a large extent, from the big-game politics of the "big shots" imprisoned in the city and its muddy, muddled modernism. How to feed the family; the problem of drought and crops; how to pay a child's school-fees; Christianity and its colonial crusade, such are the themes chosen by Head, this villager by choice sharing her pains and pleasure with her fellow human beings.

Now surprisingly, the theme of woman in relationship to man is primary in the storyteller's perspective: the community cherishes life and the continuity of the race. Not surprisingly also, Bessie Head takes sides with the woman, the silent partner whose story must be told. The bias must be expected and understood, not as the venom of a victim bent upon killing her conqueror, but as the criticism of a compatriot conscious of the necessity to reconstruct a citadel of communality through sincere sentiments and selflessness. If, as Anton Chekov has affirmed, "the aim of fiction is absolute and honest truth" (in Davis: 3), no doubt Head has fulfilled that aim. However, she has realized that there is no single truth, that truth often depends on indefinable and inevitable particularities and peculiarities, and that honesty of purpose does not always win out against the headiness of emotions. One truth that stands out in her stories is that African man has often been a monster to his woman.

Man, or the Petty Power of the Phallus

In the story, "The Collector of Treasures," Head asserts that there are two kinds of men in the society, the bad and the good, the former being in the majority. That kind

> created such misery and chaos that he could be broadly *damned* as evil. If one watched the village dogs chasing a bitch in heat, they usually moved around in packs of four or five. As the mating progressed one dog would attempt to gain dominance over the festivities and oust all the others from the bitch's vulva. The rest of the hapless dogs would stand around yapping and snapping in its face while the top dog indulged in a continuous spurt of orgasms, day and night until he was exhausted. No doubt, during the

Herculean feat, the dog imagined he was the only
penis in the world and that there had to be a
scramble for it. That kind of men lived near the
animal level and behaved just the same. Like the
dogs and bulls and donkeys, he also accepted no
responsibility for the young he procreated and
like the dogs and bulls and donkeys, he also
made females abort. (p. 91)

Now, only the hypocrite would claim to be shocked by this realistic, vivid, overwhelming imagery of man shamelessly flounting his
phallic power in the face of the hapless female victim. Of course,
the legitimate criticism of the writer would be that she has (deliberately?) neglected or negated the profound elements at play in the
creation and cultivation of this monstrous mating machine: the
village life with its boredom and monotony; the cultural and racial
factors of procreation itself; the colonial culture and its effects on
the colonized driven to existence in the vicious cycle of the bar, the
bed. But, then, the writer is not expected to make a sociological or
psychological study; she is free to use her artistic talent to exagger-
ate, to emphasize, to elucidate. If the painted picture is perturbing,
if the reflection aspect of the painter's talent.

The "dogs" in Head's stories are really awful. Such is
Gobosamang, the blind husband of Rose in the story, "Kgotla."
Rose is full of love and compassion for this heartless man that
brought her to his village from a foreign land only to take another
woman after Rose's departure for home. Rose returns and, in an
attempt to reclaim her man, finds that he is owing the new woman
a great deal of money. Gobosamang has spent it all and declares
himself unable to pay a cent. We also learn that the man took the
other woman only three months after her husband's death, which
constitutes a contravention of customs.[6] Besides, Gobosamang is
jealous and is forever believing rumours about his wife's infidelity.

There are worse men in Head's stories. They make babies
like machines and turn backs upon the poor women; hence, women
with fatherless children abound. By far, the most repulsive specimen of these irresponsible men is Garesego Mokopi, husband of
Dikeledi in "The Collector of Treasures." Educated and employed
as a clerk in the district administration service, well paid especially
with salary increment after national independence, Garesego has
all the essentials to feed his hunger for sex and alcohol: the irony
is well established by the writer, since one would have expected
such a man to be responsible and fulfill the potentials of patriotism

and responsibility. He moves from woman to woman while constantly putting his wife in the family way; one day, when the youngest of his three sons turns one, Garesego simply moves out, forever, without looking back. When, after eight years, Dikeledi goes to him for financial help in sending the first son to school, Garesego ostensibly agrees but, in reality, only out of a desire to sleep with the woman one more time. When the woman lures him to her bed and stabs him to death, the reader's first reaction is that it is a well deserved death.

The phallic as described in the Headian story, is only one aspect of a power that encompasses every element of existence in the village. The man-dog wishes to show off his total mastery in the manger and his victims are not only women, but also children. Witness the case of old man Makgobja who, convinced of the efficacy of an ancient rainmaking ceremony, sacrifices his two granddaughters, all to no avail. He is sentenced to death and one might not wish to shed a tear for him.

Not a tear, either, for Sebembele, the successor to his father as village chief who reveals that he is actually the father of the last of his father's children born by the third wife. Sebembele is forced into exile with his Rankwana and the baby and his followers are also constrained to share in the trauma of exile and alienation.

Yet -- and this is one of the supreme qualities of Bessie Head's works --, the stories leave room, call out, for a second thought whereby human understanding and compassion are brought into play. Firstly, the dog often works in concert and collusion with the bitch; the primal fascination that draws them one to the other might strike a cord of compassion in the observed. At least, the bitch is impressed. Declares the widow courted by Gobosamang:

> The trouble with Gobosamang is that he appeals
> to the heart. He is like a small child who must be
> cared for and when I saw him weeping like that,
> my heart was filled with pity and I agreed to his
> proposal and went to live with him.
> (*The Collector...* p. 66)

Even more impressed and impressive is his wife Rose -- we cannot but note the symbolic name -- who, in order to resolve the whole problem, opts to pay the man's debt in installments, from her salary. Similarly "noble gesture" (p. 67) is shown by the villagers that sympathize with old man Mokgobja's act of murder as desperate reaction to strain and suffering of starvation consequential to drought, and his attachment to a culture that has run counter to the dynamics of evolutionary process. The people

> knew in their hearts that only a hair's breadth
> had saved them from sharing a fate similar to
> that of Mokgobja's family. They could have
> killed something to make the rain fall. (p. 60)

As for Sebembele, there is even more sense in a sympathetic stance; for, by giving up the chieftaincy, he is making a choice of love over a life of lies and, indeed, his action is worthy of being emulated by others. "In a world where women were of no account, he said truthfully: 'The love between Rankwana and I is great'" (p. 3)

Sebembele's character is ample proof of the flexibility that marks Bessie Head's depiction of man and woman. He combines the dastardliness of the devil with the humanism of a true hero. In other words, Sebembele reveals some aspects of that other kind of man, "the poem of tenderness" (p. 93), presented in Head's stories. It is interesting to note that Head has stated categorically that this latter species constitutes a minority. A further remark is that the writer actually has failed to depict a truly poem-of-tenderness kind of man, the reason -- we daresay -- being that such a picture of perfection would be too fictional to maintain our (and Head's) faith in facts. The most convincing characters are those that, in spite of their goodness, remain human. An example is the man in "Snapshots of a Wedding," Kegoletile. Engaged to the educated Neo, he continues to see his illiterate girlfriend, Mathata. The latter has all the good qualities lacking in the former and, on the wedding day, Neo is urged by her aunt to "be a good wife!" (p. 80) Here, the writer uses the contrast to underscore the necessary qualities of a good woman. Realizing the need to scold the naughty, conceited, egocentric Neo (the name is again symbolic, reminding one as it does of neocolonialism), Head has carefully avoided castigating the gallavanting man.

As stated earlier, the dog and the bitch share certain characteristics and, if the dog is capable of displaying some mild-mannered behaviour, the bitch is definitely able to be bad-mannered, just as the "bad-mannered rubbish" called Neo. To further analyze the canine imagery, we recall that the bitch is a contributor, a consenter, to the dog's orgasmic drive. And it so happens that, once in a while, the bitch snatches power, dictates the terms of the contract, thus transforming the village into a sorry surrogate of the city. Such is life.

Life, or the Modernist Mania

Life is the heroine of the story of the same name. A well crafted tale, it relates the tragedy of the African woman recently returned to the village from the city. It goes deeper than the run-of-the-mill city-village dichotomy, however, for, Bessie Head uses the story to make a poignant statement on the potentially descructive forces dogging Africa's heritage. Life is a stunning, young, black beauty just back to her Botswanan village after a stint in South Africa as "singer, beauty queen, advertisement model and prostitute" (p. 38). She symbolizes the fast growing foreign culture largely conveyed by returning migrant workers. The villagers accept some of these ever increasing influences while rejecting others; they accept Life, but reject her murder by her husband.

To see her upon arrival from Johannesburg, one would never associate death with Life. She is bubbling with life, disarmingly confident, totally charming, so much so that her fellow women are fascinated by her establishing humanity's oldest profession as a business in the village. For them, Life is a heroine; even although they themselves would not dare sell their body to the best bidder, they see her as a match for the men. In their turn, the men welcome her innovation with glee. Paying her for her services reduces, indeed, removes any danger of responsibility towards girlfriends abandoned with fatherless babies. Life is quick to declare her motto:

> 'Live fast, die young, and have a good-looking
> corpse.' All that was said with the bold, free joy
> of a woman who had broken all the social ta-
> boos. (p. 40)

With her budding business comes the first hotel in the village. The women beer-brewers of the village join Life in drinking and exhibiting this seemingly new-found freedom. Suddenly, with a quick stroke of artistry, Bessie Head shows that Life is more a symbol of modern mania than the suffragist type leading her sisters to behavioral emancipation. The sentence changes the story, definitively:

> Then one evening death walked quietly into the
> bar. It was Lesego, the cattle-man. (p. 41)

At once, Life, as if destined to destruction, reveals the other side of
her persona: she is weak, impressionable, just a woman capable of
loving, and of being dominated by a strong male.

> He was the nearest thing she had seen for a long
> time to the Johannesburg gangsters she had as-
> sociated with -- the same small, economical ges-
> tures, the same power and control. (p. 41)

The fire of desire is mutual; for Lesego, normally only interested in
transient encounters, sees something special in this "new kind of
woman." He marries her upon her assurance that her "old ways are
over. I have now become a woman" (p. 42)

This last statement by Life is an eye-opener. She accepts
that her vaunted freedom is, after all, only another prison and a sad
solution to man's meanness, and that the so-called city-civilization
is but another form of dehumanization. As usual in a Bessie Head
story, and with an irony made all the more mind-boggling by
scientific and sexual coupling, like poles repel. The good woman
is forever seeking after the bad man; the good man, always attracted to the bad woman. Good women and men "seldom join
their lives together". So it is with Life and Lesego, the good and the
bad producing the tragedy of death. A further twist in the whole
logic of science translated into human irony by Bessie Head is, that
both qualities of good and evil are at once present in each of the two
protagonists of the tragic drama. Life, the prostitute, makes an
effort to "become a woman again" and Lesego, the calm one
enjoying everyone's respect, ends up being a murderer. Still, the
overwhelming fact is that, sooner than later, the couple's incom-
patability is confirmed. Lesego does not like the noise of Life's
transistor radio and, revealing the seedy side of that maleness
admired by her, he takes total control of the family-purse. In spite
of the communal culture of the village, Life cannot cope any longer.
She states: "I think I have made a mistake. Married life doesn't suit
me." (p. 44) So, when Lesego goes away briefly, "the old, reckless
wild woman awakens from a state near death with a huge sign of
relief" (p. 44) He returns home, askes her to go purchase some
sugar for tea; instead she goes to keep an appointment with a
customer. It is an appointment with death: Lesego is calm as ever,
goes to the place and stabs Life to death. The white judge calls it a

crime of passion and sentences him to five years in prison.

Now, Bessie Head has remained ambiguous about that crime. We believe that the ambiguity is an adequate comment on the very nature of the evolving society. Modernism is being espoused without proper understanding of its qualities and, as proven by Life -- both the character and the state -- the danger of destruction is as strong as the positive potentials of the new experience. The mania of modernism can only lead down the road to the cultural abyss where Africa's proud past has been buried. That the drunken village women have the last word on the saga of Life and Lesego is itself another comment on the modernist trend; for, as the repository of real culture, villagers are often too eager to imitate the been-to-the-city, thus tacitly accepting the inferiority of the culture whose preservation is being preached by some luminaries.

Villagers also support another woman, Mme-Mompati, "the patron saint" whose life proves to be just a facade for some fiendish activities, belongs to the elite, rich, humanitarian, Christian; she is "the warm-hearted, loud-voiced firm defender of all kinds of causes -- marriage morals, child care, religion, and the rights of the poor" (p. 14). When her husband, Rra-Mompati, leaves her for another woman, the whole village sympathizes with her and forces him into exile; in addition, the divorce-court grants her a handsome settlement after her great oration "to God, the Church, the Bible, the Sick, the Poor, the Suffering, the Honour of an Honourable Woman, the Blessings of Holy Matrimony and so on" (p. 15). Their son, Mompati, stays with her mother. They remain together, like "two peas in a pod" (p. 17) for ten years when Mompati takes a wife who brings about the end of Mma's influence upon the son. Then, the village loses faith in her. "The pose of God and Jesus were (sic) blown to the winds and the demented vampire behind it was too terrible to behold" (p. 18) Mother and son never see each other again.

The consolation is, that the villagers finally see through the hypocritical Mma. Bessie Head uses this story to criticize Christianity, one of the most pervasive aspects of modernist mania. However, the writer's position is not fully convincing; for, from the story-line, the woman's demise is really due to her highhandedness and too great motherly influence over Mompati. In essence, she represents better the notorious mother-in law than the hypocritical Christian. Viewed from this perspective, the story of "The Village Saint" would be considered as testimony of the triumph of love over every obstacle, as well as Head's advocacy for monog-

amy. Mompati's declaration would thus appear to be a defiance to
the vainglorious polygamist and to the meddlesome mother-in-
law: "I'm sorry, I never do anything without first consulting my
wife." (p. 18). Unfortunately, the facts of life are not that simple.
Besides, love, being a human condition and feeling, always falls
prey to many an unsavory companion, just as the human beings
themselves. The treasures of love are never immune to tragedies.

"The Collector of Treasures," or Love's Triumph and Tragedy

The story of Dikeledi in "The Collector of Treasures" is the
most significant of Head's stories. Dikeledi is sent to prison for
killing her husband. In jail, she finds four other women guilty of a
similar offense. For example, Kebonye cut off her husband's
genitals because he was too active putting school-girls in the family
way. Dikeledi's husband deserved to die, too; for, he was a sex-
maniac. In the midst of her tragic life, Dikeledi, we are told, has
always found someone to love her. "She was the collector of such
treasures." (p. 91) Briefly, Dikeledi is a good woman that arouses
positive reaction in others; apart from her husband, everybody
else, without exception, loves her. Her pregnant friend, Kenalepe,
loves her so much that she offers to tell her husband Paul to sleep
with Dikeledi and, indeed, Paul sleeps with her. The act of love is
added to the "collection of treasures."

And there is exactly the source of criticism of the whole
pack of treasures. Paul is another woman's husband, even if a
friend, and, as we have already found out, Bessie Head is an
advocate of monogamy and a critic of promiscuity. It is also
noteworthy that Kenalepe realizes the need for a man: "You ought
to find another man. It is not good for a woman to live alone." (p.
96) The tragedy of Dikeledi's life is that the man that she deserves,
"the kind of man with the power to create himself anew" (p. 93),
"the poem of tenderness," is already married. While Bessie Head
never condemns Paul, or even Dikeledi, the story does offer enough
proof of the human weaknesses of both characters. Their relationship gives room for doubt in the observer's mind and it is such a
doubt that moves Dikeledi's husband further towards his perni-
cious plan that, on the rebound, leads to his death.

The act of murder committed by Dikeledi needs further
analysis. We have asserted earlier that the reader's first reaction is,
that "the filthy pig" called Garesego deserves to die. Nonetheless,
a second assessment would be different. Dikeledi would have

added to her humanism by sparing the man's life. Paul and his wife, suspicious of their friend to the point of actually expressing a premonition of the gory event, ought to have stopped her. When Paul assures Dikeledi that he will raise her children as his own and give them an education, he only underscores the tragedy that somehow seems predetermined by destiny in Head's stories.

Other stories tell the tale of love. Jacob, hero of "Jacob: The Story of a Faith-Healing Priest," is the quintessential Christian, living in abject poverty and exhibiting an astounding selflessness, all in preparation for immortality in paradise. Jacob, son of a rich man, has lost everything. He is the contrast of another priest, Legojang, a thorough-going knave using the Word of God to hide his series of ritual murders. Lebojang is finally caught and sentenced to death, while Jacob finds peace and happiness in the arms of Johannah, a beautiful, unmarried mother of several children whom he accidentally meets in his church and to whom he claims to be directed by the Voice of God. This particular love story would appear to owe its success to prayers; however, significantly enough, the moment that he sets eye on Johannah, Jacob forgets about praying. The "dazzling light in the gloom" (p. 33) is also a woman well versed in the traditions and customs of the country. The emphasis is placed upon family, work, community, and no longer on a religion that practically imprisons man in his poverty.

The anti-Christian viewpoint expressed in Jacob's story is also seen in "Heaven is Not Closed," with the Christian woman Galethebege finding happiness with the traditionalist Ralokae. Ralokae is the symbol of protest against the imposed religion and, throughout his life, he stands firm in his conviction.

> There was something wrong with the people who had brought the word of the Gospel to the land. Their love was enslaving black people and he could not stand it ... They made people cry for love. One never had to cry for love in the customary way of life. Respect was just there for people all the time. That was why he rejected all things foreign. (pp. 9-10)

Bessie Head further stresses that Ralokae symbolizes "an ancient stream of holiness that people had lived with before the white man had set foot in the land" (p. 11). After the white missionary has excommunicated Galethebege from the church for agreeing to become a *heathen's* wife, all those villagers converted to Christianity abandon the church. The very choice made by the woman to become Ralokae's wife and do what he commands her to do, as a good wife, constitutes another protest in behalf of the established culture of the community. The writer seems to assert that the tragedies of love and life could be averted or abated if Africans blend human consideration with the basic norms of their culture. Heaven is open to Galethebege and Ralokae because they have lived in harmony and mutual respect. The man has not imposed his beliefs upon the woman. She has not allowed her Christian faith to change her priority for attaining happiness with her man.

Where such mutual consideration is absent, love loses its meaning and, the woman's quality notwithstanding, loneliness, the first step to the final tragedy, sets in. Moreover, the woman loses the respect of her people.

Conclusion: In Search of Happiness and Harmony

Both young and old are engaged in the search for happiness and love. Witness old woman Gaenametse, once a desperate drunk, now settled with her priest. "I have all I need now," she declares. "I have a good man. I am his mosadi-rra."[7] Witness the demeanour of master-hunter Tholo who over-looks the fact that his woman is already a mother and marries her because she possesses all the necessary qualities to give him a happy life. Bessie Head is realistic enough to appreciate the difficulty of realizing the ideal; hence, most of the stories in her collection recount "the incredible muddle and nonsense people make of their lives each day" (p. 109) Certain stories end on a note of ambiguity; others express a kind of fatalistic resignation, that "nothing new could be said about human nature" (p. 62). The unevenness, if such would be their description, is only another proof of the writer's realism.

Bessie Head is thus a true collector of treasures, timeless, triumphant, tragic, always human. Most importantly, she is symbolic of Africa's humanism, not the kind of bourgeois liberalism that pretends to be the voice and mirror of the people with whom it really has nothing in common. Bessie Head lived in the village and created there "new worlds out of nothing"[8] She lived on the land, as one of "the children of a real woman (who) do not get lean or die" mainly because they form a community. Head is, as we have stated, the collector of treasures.

She had the capacity to live with the conflicts of
life... Like all women, she was involved in village gossip and disputes. She knew everything,
but the richness of her communication lay in her
gift to sift and sort out all the calamities of
everyday life with the unerring heart of a good
storyteller. (pp. 108-9).

She had the courage and consciousness of the committed
and, in exile, lived through the trauma and tragedy of alienation.
If her stories, as well as her novels, are emphatic in their description
of the particular problems facing African woman, it is because the
solution of those problems are of vital importance to the ultimate
liberation of all of Africa and to the happy, harmonious co-exis-
tence of woman and man.

Indeed, Bessie Head has not been a heroine, but a human
being. As significant as the issue of male chauvinism are the
problems of christianity and materialism, aspects of the bastardiza-
tion of the heritage. Only those deliberately making partial,
prejudiced assessment of her works would restrict the scope of the
headian thematic horizon. In her literary universe, her sentiment
does not deteriorate into sentimentality. Bias for the female species
does not lead to blackmail of the male. The hurt of being a woman
and living her womanhood neither becomes hate for man nor
matches the horror in the face of that madness called apartheid.

Notes

[1] Bessie Head, *The Collector of Treasures*, London: Heinemann, 1977, p. 106.

[2] *Ibid.*, p. 46

[3] *Ibid.*, p. 30

[4] As the foremost South African black female writer, she has retained well merited attention of critics of African writers, particular the female species. See, among others:

L. Lyold W. Brown, *Women Writers in Black Africa*, Westport: Greenwood Press, 1981;

Mineke Schipper, ed, *Unheard Words ...*, London: Allison and Busby, 1984; Eldred D. Jones et al, eds., *Women in African Literature Today*, London: James Currey Ltd., 1987.

[5] Robert Gorham Davis, ed., *Ten Modern Masters*, New York: Harcourt Brace Jovanovich, 1972, p. 5.

[6] In the average African society, the widow/widower must mourn for one year after the partner's death before taking a new one.

[7] *The Collector of Treasures*, p. 86. The word means, "the special one".

[8] Interview in *Ms* magazine, 4, 5 (Nov. 1975), p. 73.

Narrative Strategies in Bessie Head's Stories

H. Nigel Thomas

Today one almost feels the need to apologize for analyzing the works of writers like Bessie Head, Chinua Achebe, Buchi Emecheta, Ngugi Wa Thiongo, and most other African writers. For if one is to follow recent trends in criticism, one should not be looking at how fiction conveys truths lost in the diffuseness of reality, rather one should be hypothesizing about metafiction and postmodernism, that is to say, preoccupying one's self with finding critical theories to account for the literature created by those whom we are told are at the "cutting edge" of literary creation because they manage to unsay everything they have said, manage to deconstruct the fictive universe which more often than not they have not yet constructed. Thus, those who have been crowned deans of contemporary literary criticism would have us believe that our time should be spent deriving meaning from a process that cannot mean; for —and in this they are mostly correct— "postmodernist literature" is about the meaning of non-meaning. This approach is certainly well-suited to a civilization that can no longer believe anything, to cultures where language has lost its bonding quality principally because language has become a mask concealing the feared unknown in the other.

When we turn to African societies, we witness ferment everywhere, much of it very disconcerting. But instead of reproducing chaos and deforming reality and syntax to reproduce this ferment, the vast majority of African writers use language to contruct verbal laboratories with which to probe chaos and discover its implications. If one compares the non-fiction and fiction of Bessie Head, one discovers very quickly that Head's fiction is an intensification, a distillation, if you will, of Botswana history and actuality in order to suggest its impact of those who live it. Indeed, her collection of testimonials from Serowe residents on subjects ranging from history to contemporary medical practice economics, in *Serowe: Village of the Rain Wind*, is a handy source of the raw materials that Head reworked — and never distorted — in order to create her four novels and collection of short stories. It is evident from Head's handling of her themes that her concern in writing fiction was to praise what she deemed praiseworthy, condemn what she saw as oppressive, and highlight what she saw as social folly. In a Voice of America interview, she told Lee Nichols:

> "... I would never fall in the category of a writer who produces light entertainment .... My whole force and direction comes from having something to say. What we are mainly very bothered about has been the dehumanizing of black people. And if we can resolve these situations—and I work both within the present and future—if we can resolve our difficulties it is because we want a future which is defined for our children. So then we can't sort of say that you have ended any specific thing or that you have changed the world. You have merely offered your view of a grander world, of a world that's much grander than the one we've had already" (1981, 55-56).

This is essentially the vision of a bard. It follows, therefore, that Head's fictions is didactic but only, for the most part, implicitly so. Her approach is not to obscure the subjects she writes about, or to leave interpretation strictly up to the reader, but rather to clarify without being reductive or simplistic. In fact, all her short stories reflect a complex awareness of human nature and human motives. Some of them, like *The Collector of Treasures, Looking for a Rain God*, and *Life*, achieve the status of tragedy in the Aristotelian sense of the twin emotion they evoke—fear and pathos.

The narrative strategies authors of fiction choose are determined primarily by their themes and intentions and secondarily by writers' knowledge of fictive technique. We already know, from the citation from The Voice of America interview, why Head wrote fiction. But what determined her technique? I think that the oral origins of much of the material she reworked into fiction affected her technique profoundly. The material simply imposed itself. The tales have as their central concern Serowe village life, and in this they resemble the folktale cycles, embodying several stories about a single protagonist. In creating fiction from the oral accounts of the tribe, Head transforms herself into something of a literary griot; we have already seen that the task she sets herself gives her a bardic role. Both of these roles imply a particular treatment in the interpretation of the material. The griot recounts in a historical fashion and it is important that s/he enter the minds of his/her characters to reveal their thoughts and motivations. The bard is interested in the lessons s/he can draw from the past so that s/he can interpret the present and predict the future. Implicit in the bardic approach, therefore, is copious commentary, interpretation, if you will, of the forces impinging on the characters' actions.

To the foregoing one needs to add the fact that Head received her formal education in South Africa, and therefore in the Western tradition. Certainly, we see from her first forays into writing fiction that she had already mastered fictive technique—her arrangement of the episodes in *When Rain Clouds Gather* for their dramatic effect and her transformation of the awaited rain and the setting into symbols are masterly done. Hence, what we are to understand is that Head combined Western literary and African storytelling methods in writing the stories—she calls them tales very advisedly—that comprise *The Collector of Treasures*. One very evident Western technique in these stories is her conflation of history and several oral accounts into single stories

As I have mentioned already, the arrangement of the stories contributes to their meanings. A quick summary of the themes the stories cover will be in order. In general the stories are about the failure of colonial civilisation and the perennial oppression of women in Botswana society (for a profound analysis of the latter in Head's novels, see Ola, 1986). More specific themes are: the defiance of tribal custom in asserting individuality where only communally-sanctioned behaviour is permitted; psychological turmoil resulting from the conflict between Christian and indigenous practices and beliefs; the motives behind the creation of indigenous Christianity; the inevitable erosion of communal values when they come into contact with urban vice; the debilitating impact of deep-rooted beliefs in witchcraft; the triumphing of the irrational (regression) in times of deep duress; the wisdom inherent in the communal courts (kgotla); the lethal elements of consumer values; the advantages of traditional over European marriage rituals; the limits of mask-wearing; the social disintegration that follows the dissolution of the mores of a society; the victimization of women and children in a society where no firmly enforced codes exist for their protection. All the foregoing themes are touched upon explicitly or implicitly in the first two stories of the collection. The first story reveals tribal fracturing resulting from individual initiative, showing what Head felt was a weakness of tribal organization; it also shows the insufficiency of tribal law to regulate human emotions; it equally reveals the ritualization of prejudice against the female sex, since it is women who are blamed for the fragmenting of the tribe. Head chooses and arranges the events of this story to show how, under tribal governments, people are prohibited from cultivating individuality; she thus prepares us, as it were, to understand the void males experience when, following independence, they are required to display initiative but find that they possess none. The second story introduces us to the Christian Church in action, the contempt its missionaries hold for those members of the community who are not members of the Botswana aristocracy, and thus indirectly shows us one reason why several people do not take the teachings of Christianity seriously, why indigenous churches spring up, why beliefs in witchcraft remain unassailable, and why in times of crises people look to the ancestors for answers rather than to reason for solutions.

Turning to the oral sources of these stories, we find Head signalling to us from the beginning of the collection that much of the material in her stories is derived from oral sources. The first story is an etiological tale, derived from oral history. All the marks of the folktale are present: an omniscient narrator, copious summary, reduction of motives to a few primary ones, as well as a moral. The tale itself, however, is intended to condemn women for the suffering of the tribe; Head narrates it so that tribal hegemony at the expense of individual expression (creating a child-like obedience in the populace) is the real culprit. It is an excellent example of the material itself being rearranged so that the traditional view is presented and at the same time undermined, a combination of oral an literary techniques.

The oral sources of the stories or the influence of the oral forms of storytelling are evident in the beginning of Head's stories. One gets a formula that suggests the following decision: Now this story happened in a place called X. Let me describe that place for you before I tell you the story. This is the case with the story "Jacob: The Story of a Faith Healing Priest." In "Heaven is not Closed," there are two narrators: one is Head, providing the setting for the story; the other is an oral story teller that tells the story of Galathebege's life-long struggle to choose between Christian and Botswana customs and beliefs to the audience of mourners. The second narrator reports the audience's responses to the story. Another example of the oral influence is Head's need to give a resumé of the story in the first paragraph. For example, in "Heaven is not Closed," Head begins the story as follows, "all her life

Gathethebege earnestly believed that her whole heart ought to be devoted to God, although one catastrophe after another occurred to deflect her from this path. It was only in the last five years of her life, after her husband, Ralokae, and died, that she was able to devote her whole mind to her calling...." The paragraph goes on to complete the summary of the story. When this is not the case, the stories begin, like the oral historian describing the life and times of a particular personage before recounting his deeds, by informing us of the forces to which the particular protagonist is reacting. This is not to say the Head does not make this presentation of setting— social, historical, or physical—interesting. Often, as in the present example, this filling in of background or the presentation of sum- mary is graphically executed. Whey they contribute to the organic or the intellectual unity of the story, as I shall show later, the authorial intrusions are successful, even indispensable. The oral influences in Head's fiction are also evident in the closure of the stories, which more often than not, express the moral of the story. This is especially noticeable in "The Wind and a Boy, which ends as follows, "And thus progress, development, and a pre-occupation with status and living standards first announced themselves to the village. It looked like being an ugly story with many decapitated bodies on the main road" (p. 75).

Serowe: Village of the Rain Wind is an excellent tool for the examination of Head's technique of conflating several incidents into a single story. The first story of the collection is a brilliant example of this process. It is an evocation of ancient migrations as well as nineteenth and twentieth century political crises: the crises over Khama the Great's conversion to Christianity and his conse- quent abandonment of certain ethnic practices, resulting in battles between him and his father and uncle and a fragmenting of the tribe; Tshekedi Khama's own migration to avoid a full-fledged war with his nephew Seretse on account of latter's marriage outside the tribe (See Serowe, pp. 3-18, 77, 95). Although Head discusses the Mfecane—a series of interethnic wars that raged on for close to twenty years in the region (See Serowe, 180-182)—she excludes war from this story. The reason is that Head felt that the migrations had been "established over the centuries to avert bloodshed in a crisis;" this tendency she saw as "underlying the basic non-violent nature of African society as it was then. This gives the lie to white historians, who for their own ends, damned African people as sav- ages" (Serowe, 95). Thus, in "The Deep River River: A Story of Ancient Tribal Migration,: Head conflates an excludes in accor- dance with her vision of the true nature of African people.

The second story in the collection, "Heaven Is not Closed," also illustrates quite well Head's technique of conflation. The story explores the psychic dislocation resulting from Khama the Great's policies in imposing Christianity on the entire society. This problem, which created warfare and much tribal fracturing, is examined in "Heaven Is not Closed " for the divided loyalties and religious incertitude Khama's policies created. The arrogance of the early missionaries and their *a priori* contempt for everything that was non-European are juxtaposed with the indigenous pride some Botswana felt for their customs. Head's reason for distilling various stories to arrive at this core and for structuring the elements in this particular way is to show the extent to which the early Christian missionaries alienated the population, notwithstanding Khama's imposition of Christianity on the Batswana people (the core of the story exists in one of the reminiscences included in *Serowe: Village of the Rain Wind* (see pp. 30-31)). While Head felt a deep admiration for Khama, she nonetheless had strong views about the consequences of his Christianization policy:

> When I think of Khama's conversion to Christianity and his imposition of it on the tribe as a whole— it more or less forced him to modify or abolish all the ancient customs of his people, thus stripping them of certain securities which tradition offered. ... People might have not realized this, and this might account for the almost complete breakdown of family life in Bamangwato country, which under traditional custom was essential for the survival of the tribe (Serowe, xiv-xv)

Head's compression technique sometimes assumes the form of symbol. This is the case in "The Wind and the Boy," where Robinson the protagonist exemplifies potential strength created from intelligence, resourcefulness, and a blending of the eclectic from all traditions, while his killer, the driver of the brakeless automobile, exemplifies the reckless, who give themselves value by acquiring Western modes of existence the deadly power of which they do not understand.

It is in the contrasting structure of some of Head's stories (as well as in their arrangement in the collection) that her perception of herself as a writer in the bardic tradition is best revealed. "The Collector of Treasures" and "Jacob: The Story of a Faith Healing Priest," are particularly useful for this discussion. "The Collector of

Treasures" is the story in which Head probes at her deepest the breakdown of family structure in Botswana. Head's intention is to show how promiscuity on the part of the men deprives the nation of a vast part of its human resources. Basic to the story's structure are two families: one that should be headed by Mokopi, except that he drinks and whores away his civil service salary; the other, that of Paul Kebolo, a responsible man, whose wife is happy, well-adjusted woman, with an overwhelming generosity to others. Mokopi's wife is a talented woman: "she could knit, sew, and weave baskets" (*Collector*, 90) but she must raise three children all by herself.

This story is one of the best-realized in the collection. Its artistic success is due partly to its theme but more so to Head's use of contrast (a technique that accounted in large measure for the brilliant artistry of her earlier work: *When Rain Clouds Gather*). Paul Kebolo's responsibility in providing for his family and still having enough to help along Mokopi's wife is contrasted with Mokopi's spending his money on sex and alchohol. Paul's compassion for Dikeledi is contrasted with Mokopi's conviction that you only feed a woman's children if that woman is your mistress. Such compassion also stands out against Mokopi's understanding of money as a weapon to be used in humiliating those dependent on him for it, in this case his wife. Mokopi's hopping from bar to bar and bed to bed is contrasted with Paul's transformation of his home into a centre where thinking people can discuss political and social issues. Finally Kenapele's happiness, because Paul does not evade any of his marital responsibilities, is contrasted with Dikeledi's initial stoicism and unhappiness and eventual imprisonment.

At the end of the story Paul Kebolo adopts Dikeledi's three children and promises to provide them with a secondary education; for upon realizing that Mokopi had come to her home merely to humiliate her, Dikeledi castrates and simultaneously murders him. Thus the trauma created by male irresponsibility has to be palliated by others already shouldering their own responsibility. The tone of Head's commentary in the story is an angry one. She likens men like Mokopi to bulldogs and jackasses, who, their sexual pleasure ended, have no responsibility toward their off-spring (more will be said about the authorial commentary in this story in that section of the essay reserved for it). The ramifications of male parental irresponsibility is Head's principal concern in writing this story. A secondary theme, embodied in the other half of the story's dialectic, is the somewhat Herculean task of the responsible parents, who in addition to raising their own children, must raise the abandoned children too. Elsewhere Head tells us that ninety-seven percent of the children born in Serowe are out of wedlock and that most of them "will never know who their real father is" (Serowe, 58). In this same article Head blames the blanket imposition of Christianity on the population and the indifference of colonial government to the tribal mores it destroyed for the moral void created among Botswana males (pp. 58-61). In one of the four testimonials regarding the breakdown of Botswana family life included in *Serowe: Village of the Rain Wind*, Lebang Moreni, age 18, states that men deny that they are fathers of the children to avoid paying child support. When they are made to pay, they sometimes leave the village. If they remain they sporadically provide a fraction of the amount required, and the law courts lack the will to enforce its sanctions. Such support, however, is limited only to the first child. A woman who already has a child cannot expect the law to force the father(s) to subsequent children to support them.

> Many, many women are now rearing children on their own and it is not a good life. Children see one man after another calling on their mother and they lose all respect for her. Our children run wild, are very cheeky and have become thieves. Most of the thefts which now take place in Serowe are done by small boys. They raid houses for money, cigarettes or food. Theft was never a part of our life. I had a father and I know what a beating meant for bad behaviour (pp. 64-65).

"The Collector of Treasures" is a dramatized compression of such testimony as well as Head's ideas on the consequences of child abandonment by Botswana fathers. Head continues the same theme, though not with the same degree of contrast—for the emphasis is on responsible men choosing their spouses—in the story "Hunting."

Whereas Head's use of contrast in "The Collector of Treasures" heightens the story's artistry, an attempt at a similar structuring in "Jacob: The Story of a Faith-Healing Priest" produces a colossal failure. In the latter there are two separate stories, each a version of, and a judgment on, the extreme motivations that give rise to the faith-healing churches. Because Head fails to integrate the actions of both of the main characters the story is truncated. By spending some two pages on a setting that is of no relevance to the theme of the story (this is a case where oral story telling conditioning is an impediment) and by grafting a romance of very limited value on to it, the focus of the story is diffuse. In "The Collector of Treasures" it is rare that the narrative departs from Dikeledi. She provides the narrative pivot. In "Jacob: The Story of a Faith Healing Priest" Jacob does not provide enough of that focus.

The aspect of Head's narrative approach likely to be most controversial is her constant intrusion in her own voice in the stories. I support that Head felt that in order for her readers to appreciate the behaviour of characters like Mokopi, Life, and Mma Mabele, she needed to provide the social background of these characters. Because this information is not implicit in the drama- tized action of the stories, they sometimes evince an essayistic (expository) quality. My feeling regarding these interventions is that Head wanted them there and chose to hold on to the oral story telling model of sketching in background whenever it is deemed necessary for a better understanding of the story being told. In Head's case, such intrusions can be a vital dimension of the story. In these stories, one simply has to see the author's presence in the story in the manner one accepts some playwrights' creation of a stage narrator whose purpose is to put events in their proper perspective. Wayne Booth tells us that it is usual for critics to condemn commentary in fiction. But Booth goes on to invite literary critics to "at the very least... decide with some precision whether any of the particular achievements of the author's voice have been worth the sacrifice of whatever principles we hold dear" (1961, 169). We need only look at Melville's *Billy Budd*, where commentary is vital to *peripetia*, operates in lieu of direct characteri- zation of Billy Budd, and presents the novella's historic setting—for confirmation of the validity of Booth's advice. For we have accorded *Billy Budd* classic status.

We could appreciate the value of the intrusions by removing them and examining the difference such alterations makes to the meaning of the stories. Most of them would diminish in signifi- cance. It is also easy to see that entire novels or novellas would have been required to dramatize much of the information that Head provides in summary form in her own voice. If one function of art is to compress for effect, then, here the use of authorial commentary is justified.

The main reason for the authorial commentaries of Head's short fiction is to provide social setting, which, in these stories, is as vital as the background colours a painter chooses for his paintings. It is because of these settings that we understand the mores that inhibit or incite the characters. As I have already mentioned, in the

West, a basic feature of the short story is the assumption that the writer and reader belong to a similar cultural mosaic and hence bring a similar value scheme to creation and creative interpretation. Head could make no similar assumption, for her characters are fundamentally non-Western.

A close look at the story "Life" will show the foregoing in operation. The first paragraph of the story tells us in Head's own voice that village people rejected whatever they considered harmful and absorbed whatever they considered beneficial. "The murder of Life had this complicated undertone of rejection" (*Collector*, 37). When we later discover that Life is a prostitute, an unknown occupation in the village, our emotions intensify, but only because Head has already told us in her own voice that Life's return to the village was necessitated by the recall of all Botswana citizens from South Africa in 1963, the year when formal boundaries were established between South Africa and Botswana in preparation for the latter's independence. During the seventeen years Life had lived in Johannesburg she developed into a prostitute. On her own, we know that she would never have returned to the village.

Irony is achieved in the story partly through Head's ironic naming of the character, but moreso because Head tells us of the community's expectations of Life. "'She is going to bring us a little light,' the women said among themselves as they went off to fetch their work tools." Head's commentary reads as follows: "They were always looking 'for the light' and by that they meant that they were ever alert to receive new ideas that would freshen up the ordinariness and everydayness of village life" (p. 38). Life brings a Luciferan light to the community. Her companions eventually are not the light seekers: they abandon her; rather they are the pariahs: the beer brewers, who vicariously admire her for turning the tables, for making me pay for sex. In this respect she teaches the community something for hitherto women were the ones exploited in sex; for the first time women see that they could make men pay for sex and could in this fashion wield power over them. The attempt to force the community's mores on her, to cure her of the urban sickness of prostitution, through marriage, fails. It results in her murder and her husband's imprisonment. There is light in that too: that once the values of the city enter, communal mores are unable to neutralize them. Without Head's commentary we could not appreciate the significance of the drama and irony inherent in this story.

To conclude, it is evident from Head's short stories that one of her principal concerns was an understanding on the reader's part of the social forces determining the actions of her characters. Where the events of the story do not fully imply what those social forces are, she provides them in her own voice. This practice, along with the retention of some of the traits of the oral sources of the stories, makes the stories appear different from typical twentieth century short stories in the Western tradition. I suspect that, faced with the question of her departure from standard short story practice, Head would have been interested in whether the reader understood the stories, was moved by them, and was instructed by them. In my own case the answer is yes. Her reply would be, "Well it is because of all those rules that you accuse me of breaking."

Works Cited

Achebe, Chinua. *Morning Yet on Creation Day.* London: Heinemann, 1975.

Booth, Wayne. *The Rhetoric of Fiction.* Chicago & London: The University of Chicago Press, 1961.

Head, Bessie. *The Collector of Treasure and Other Botsawana Village Tales.* London: Heinemann, 1977.

_____. *Serowe: Village of the Rain Wind.* London: Heinemann, 1981.

_____. Interview with Lee Nichols. In *Conversations with African Writers: Interviews with Twenty-Six African Authors.* Edited by Lee Nichols. Washington, D.C.: Voice of America, 1981.

Ola, Virginia U. "Women's Role in Bessie Head's Ideal World.: ARIEL 17: 4 (October 1986), 39-47..

wa Thiong'o, Ngugi. *Decolonising the Mind: The Politics of Language in African Literature.* London: James Currey, 1986.

Waugh, Patricia. *Metafiction: The Theory and Practice of Self-Conscious Fiction..* London: Methuen, 1984.

Imagery in Bessie Head's Work

Horace I. Goddard

Bessie Head, Southern Africa's profoundest and most intense woman writer, explores the meaning of an outcast's life from the vantage point of an exile from her native South Africa . Living in neighbouring Botswana enabled her to examine in minute detail the religious, social and political implications of the state of being an outcast.

In one form or another, the women in her novels are outcasts. In *Maru*, Margaret, the artist, brings together all the traumas of her exilic status and focuses them artistically in her paintings, where she brings order out of chaos. Out of the deficiencies of nature, she brings to bear a wholeness that is evidenced in the way she patterns her life, with the hope of gaining inner moral strength and outward social integrity.

A Question of Power presents Elizabeth in a disorientated state. It also reflects the fears and struggles of "self" in a world that denies the outcast a personal identity. One may argue that in *Maru* and in *A Question of Power* the protagonists are types that symbolize the forces of good and evil in a co-existential relation.

Evil and good are archetypal and controlling images an provide some kind of unity to the plots of both novels. It is through analysis of these polar, yet unified forces, that Head challenges the reader to examine his own being and the world around him. These two novels contain multidimensional themes, such as the nature of brotherhood, power worship, African racialism, identity and personal survival, which explore the nature of man within the confines of the world that he creates or that is created for him. In *A Question of Power*, for example, we are taken into the inner recesses of Elizabeth's mind where the quest for power is not a megalomaniacal attempt to exert control over territory or political decision-making, but where there is a subtle attempt to subvert and possess a person's soul. This struggle for Elizabeth's soul, by the forces of good and evil, becomes one of the unifying elements of the novel.

In *Maru*, one of the unifying components is the dream with its multiplex meanings, and through which the gods speak to the protagonist, Maru. The novel hinges on his "haunting fear that he would one day be forced to kill Moleka, one way or another."[1] This fear comes to head in the intrigues and antagonism that emerge between these close friends as they rival each other for the love of the Bushwoman, Margaret Cadmore.   The rivalry mirrors the forces of good and evil in their intensity, and portrays Moleka as Maru's alter ego in his evil aspect. Maru outwits Moleka to get the Masarwa to be his woman. When Moleka offers Margaret a bed to sleep on, it is Maru who orders it removed. The intensity of this rivalry culminates in a revenge plot in which Moleka impregnates Maru's sister, Dikeledi. This is precisely what Maru wants, for it enables him to leave with Margaret, fulfilling the ironic statement he made to Moleka: "One day we will part over a woman." (*Maru*, p. 37).   The parting is important; it is a spiritual and physical separation for Maru and Margaret.   They become initiates in the ritual for survival in their far removed dreamland where they will repeat the cycle of exilic living. Maru's departure is linked to his dream of an escape to a world where decency, tolerance and justice exist. This Utopian world is linked ostensibly to the forces of good. It is also symbolically linked to the field of daisies that Maru planted.

The floral image in the novel is one of its controlling motifs. The flowers represent the two extremes of human existence -- life and death. In particular, the daisy, the "eye of the day," resembles the sun, and is associated with vitality, sustenance and by extension, life and goodness. On another symbolic level, the flowers foreshadow a break with an evil past for Maru and Margaret and point to a new beginning where goodness, it is hoped, will be supreme. In act, when Maru and Margaret escape as man and wife, they leave behind the stymied world of oppression, brutality and petty chieftaincy. In the end, Margaret becomes an insider of sorts, but it is ironic that both she and her husband are destined to repeat the cycle of exile to fulfil their dreams of human decency within the brotherhood of man. Margaret's dream is therefore significant to the vision of liberation and a new dawn which are indicated in the novel.

The dream is so important to the fabric of the novel, *Maru*, that it is worth setting down for closer scrutiny and analysis:

> I saw the pitch black clouds envelop the sky, but
> when I looked at my feet the whole field was filled

with yellow daisies. They stirred a little as though
they were dancing. Their movement also created
this effect of gently revolving light. The next
moment I was surprised to find myself walking
along a footpath between the lovely daisies. I
looked up again and a little way ahead I saw two
people embrace each other. I stared quite hard because they were difficult to see. Their forms were
black like the house and the sky, out, again, they
were surrounded by this yellow light. I felt so
ashamed, thinking I had come upon a secret which
ought not to be disclosed, that I turned and tried to
run away. Just then a strong wind arose and began
to blow me in the direction of the embracing
couple. I was terrified. They did not want anyone
near them and I could feel it. I dropped to the
ground and tried to grab hold of the daisies to save
myself from the strong wind. At that moment I
opened my eyes. The funny thing was, this happened again and again until I put the pictures
down on paper. (*Maru*, p. 103)

I would not attempt to use Freudian dream analysis to
unravel the dream since African cosmology is enough to explain its
significance. To the African, the world is one everchanging and yet
unified whole. Good and evil are viewed as opposite ends of the
same continuum. These basic notions will help us to examine more
closely the the symbols in the dreams which fall into two categories
-- darkness and light. The "black clouds" are miraculously transformed to fields of "yellow daisies", stirring as in a dance. The
change from a cosmic to terrestrial form links the heaven and earth.
Similarly, the dancer leaping from the earth into the air, connects
yet again two opposite spheres in the physical world of nature.

The elements such as the wind, the clouds and the ground,
in their changing forms, symbolize the political decisions that are
imminent, and that will force Maru to abnegate his political responsibilities for a more compassionate way of life. Maru's transformation is bound up with the controlling gods within him, and who
shape his destiny. This life reflects the ambivalence of good and
evil and the constant struggle of one force to dominate the other.
Maru is a dreamer, a schemer and a pervert. He is harsh, cruel,
beautiful, tender and affectionate. Eventually, good is made to
triumph over evil in his character.

Margaret, on the other hand, is steadfast in her purpose and in her vision. She is "not ashamed of being a Masarwa." (p.24). This acceptance of "self" provides a measure of strength for her people people who are ostracized and dehumanized by other Africans and Europeans alike. However, Margaret refuses to live the lie of being thought of as "mixed breed" or Cape-coloured, and declares her true identity as a Masarwa.

Bessie Head, through her principal female characters, forces the African Black man to examine his relationship towards Black women. In *Maru*, Margaret thus becomes a symbol of motherhood and one of female liberation and power. Head writes about a liberation not only from a colonial past but also from the African male's racialistic, sexist and power-seeking tendencies. She exhorts the African man to cast off those rigid, false, social systems of class and caste which encumber him and deny others their humanity. This proselytizing for some sort of new saving grace is expressed towards the end of the novel, and is summed up by the Masarwas in their reaction to Maru's and Margaret's marriage:

> The wind of freedom, which was blowing through-out the world for all people, turned and flowed into the room. As they breathed in the fresh, clear air their humanity awakened...They started to run into the sunlight, then they turned and looked at the dark, small room. They said: "We are not going back there." (p. 126)

The liberation frees the Masarwa people from a physical and psychological "prison" which is confining, stultifying and dark. The "dark, small room" is symbolic of that world. On the other hand "the sunlight" which is the other unifying image in the novel, triumphs over the darkness. I would argue that the novel demonstrates the need for both prevailing forces of light and darkness, good and evil, even though, in the end, good is exalted over evil.

There is a strong religio-mythic dimension in *Maru* which is linked to the redemption and salvation of the Masarwa, but there is also a reversal of fortunes. Margaret, the outcast, becomes an insider and the insider Maru becomes and outcast from his people. Eventually, both become the harbingers of a new order in a land "a thousand miles away where the sun rose, new and new and new each day." (p. 125). This Utopic never-never land is their ultimate paradise where the golden, life-sustaining sun never sets. The obverse of this world is explored in Bessie Head's third novel, *A Question of Power*.

In *Maru*, Margaret Cadmore, the Masarwa, is brought up by an English white woman by the same name. In *A Question of Power*, Elizabeth is the daughter of a white woman who breeds for a black stable hand. She is abandoned and lives with an Asian family and later in a German foster home. Elizabeth is an outcast and does not fit into the world of whites or blacks; she is an aberration. At school she is ill-treated by the children; the principal also ostracizes her. This early pattern on the plot indicates that a *A Question of Power* is a sequel to *Maru*. It deals in depth with many of the themes and issues raised in its precursor. Elizabeth has similar experiences to Margaret: two men fight for the possession of her soul, she is despised, feels persecuted and is manipulated by the men around her. Her outcast status among the Botswana renders her "an out-and-out outsider" who "would never be in on their things."[2] That she suffers severe mental illness is not surprising. She is perpetually haunted by Sello and Dan, the first a resident of Motabeng whom she has never met and the other, a figment of her fertile imagination. Through the "wild-eyed" Greek mythological character, Medusa, the novelist probes the depth of Elizabeth's inner consciousness. By way of dreams, imaginings and phantasmagoric musings, we get an understanding of those things that torment her. What we often see are opposing forces of madness and sanity and good and evil which vie for the possession of her soul.

The controlling images mentioned above correspond with those of light and darkness in *Maru*. Always, these forces tend to redefine the identity of the protagonists. Elizabeth is the castaway heroine of *A Question of Power*, and represents the novelist's struggle against an Africa which is "shut in and exclusive." (p. 38). Elizabeth's psychoses are those of Africa. Head reminds us repeatedly that Africa's leaders are repugnant and vicious; they despise the masses:

> They don't view the African masses as having any dignity or grandeur. They're just illiterates who don't know anything, so they think they can get up there and steal and cheat and squander money. (*A Question of Power*, p. 133)

Bessie Head chooses Elizabeth to be the primal sufferer, and her suffering becomes archetypal. The image of woman as mother, procreator and guardian of the race is subverted by men who are portrayed as devoid of "love", "tenderness" and the "personal, romantic treasuring of women." (p. 137). In this torpid society, power is maintained through the forces of evil, witchcraft and oppression. There is a sustained pressure of mental torture that reduces the victims to a state of permanent madness..

There is a terror in Elizabeth's soul that is reflected in the personages of Sello and Dan. Her lapses into and out of the inner world of her mind and the external world of Botswana society depict a mental configuration which constantly reflects the revolving sides of good and evil, light and darkness, God and devil, madness and sanity. Like Maru, Elizabeth is driven by the gods within who compete for her soul. Her gods emerge from every major religion and civilization to people the canvas of her mind, as did the gods of Yorubaland on Kola's giant canvas in Soyinka's *The Interpreters*.

Elizabeth's own struggle to maintain a personal identity is linked to the godhead. Sello and Dan are projections of the anomaly that is Elizabeth; she is neither black nor white, neither European nor African. Existing as a "non-person" is an aberration to the African, for existence itself can only be explained within a world of good or evil. Her existential dilemma is expressed in her declarations to Sello and Dan:

> I'm not the dog of the Africans, you hear? I'm not
> the dog of these bastard Botswana, do you hear?
> It's you, you and Dan. You are so weak you don't
> care where you put your penis. Why must I be the
> audience of shit. (p.175)

Her hatred for this macho African male power is more forcefully expressed in her protestation to Dan:

> I'm not an African. Don't you see? I never want to
> be an African. You bloody well, damn well leave
> me alone! (p.181)

Bessie Head's statement in this novel is that man is basically evil and corrupt. The juxtaposition of light and darkness reveals a propensity for either of these forces. Power is obviously equated with darkness and evil and light with goodness. As the novel closes Kenosi, a person of 'light', sits with Elizabeth and sips tea at the table. "The darkness fell upon them and still they sat dreaming in the light of two candles on the table." (p.205) The light, as in *Maru*, signals a "New dawn" and a "new world" order for Elizabeth. She now accepts that

> She had fallen from the very beginning into the warm embrace of the brotherhood of man, because when people wanted everyone to be ordinary it was just another way of saying man loved man. As she fell asleep, she placed one soft hand over her land. It was a gesture of belonging. (p.206)

The transformation from rebelliousness to acceptance, from an outcast status to an insider, from darkness to light, has that redemptive quality about it. But, ironically, the light is a dim light which is ominous and points to its destructive nature.

Both novels castigate the evil of corrupting power, human denigration and the forces of darkness. Their controlling and unifying images are those of light and darkness, with their associated meanings. In the end, light predominates, but Bessie Head makes us fully aware that it is only the human soul which, acting as a torch or beacon, can keep the forces of evil in check.

Notes

1 Bessie Head, *Maru* (London Heinemann Educational Books Ltd., African Writers Series, 1982), p. 8.
2 Bessie Head, *A Question of Power* (London: Heinemann Educatinal Books Ltd., African Writers Series, 1985), p. 26.

The Fairy Tale and the Nightmare

Daniel Gover

In her first two novels, *When Rain Clouds Gather* and *Maru*, Bessie Head depicts love as a magical force from a fairy tale that overcomes insurmountable obstacles and unites people of different cultures and classes. This dream pattern of love is abruptly shattered in her third novel, *A Question of Power*. In this apocalyptic work, the breakdown of a woman's sanity is caused by the destructive sexuality and torture of men. Though this story may seem to be the exact opposite of the first two novels, it is the theme of power and powerlessness that creates the link between the fairy tale of love and the nightmare of sexual torture.

Maru is the story of racial prejudice conquered by idealistic love functioning as a socially progressive force that advances mankind in the direction of racial equality. It is also the story of the competition of two men for one woman. The African princes Moleka and Maru are both in love with a young Bushwoman, Margaret Cadmore, but interestingly, she does not choose between the two. In fact she is only indirectly aware that Moleka is even interested in her. Instead, she becomes the prize in the traditional rivalry and power struggle that already exists between the two men. Only toward the end does Maru inform his sister Dikeledi that he intends to marry Margaret. For most of the story, therefore, Margaret is unaware that she is going to be rescued by one of these future chiefs.

But her need to be rescued becomes apparent when the forces of evil direct their hatred at her. When she begins her job as a primary school teacher in the remote Botswana village of Dilepe, her education, manners and accent lead village people to consider her a "coloured" person, the child of a mixed race marriage, rather than a Masarwa, the derogatory term equivalent to "nigger" that many Botswana use to refer to the Bushmen. Having been raised by a white missionary's wife, Margaret has been sheltered from the sense of racial inferiority that Bushmen are subject to in Botswana.

When she reveals her racial identity, the village powers act against her. Her school principal incites her class to drive her from the room by chanting, "You are a Bushman." Initially she is saved by another teacher, Dikeledi, Maru's sister who is herself in love with Moleka. But the forces of evil are not so easily defeated. They reside in three important village totems of power; the school principal, the education supervisor and Maru's younger brother, a chief's son who practices cattle stealing like most chiefs. They represent the traditional forces of reactionary tribal power that rest on the slave labor of Bushmen, that are now threatened by an independent educated Bushman teacher like Margaret. But she can only be saved from these strong forces by the intervention of a hero who is motivated by love. And his love must be so pure that it can refine even his own nature, as both chiefs Moleka and Maru are the owners of Bushmen slaves. So her two would-be lovers must pass the test of overcoming their own racial prejudice if they are to prove worthy of rescuing the heroine.

This test of the two heroes takes an interesting form. Moleka is the first to fall in love with Margaret but is in need of the most reforming. He is widely known as a great womanizer in the village, and his passion for love is regarded as sexually dangerous, even violent: "There was nothing Moleka did not know about the female anatomy. It made him arrogant and violent. There was no woman who could resist the impact of his permanently boiling blood-stream" (*Maru*, 35). His male sexual power has always proven destructive to women: "Moleka and women were like a volcanic explosion in a dark tunnel. Moleka was the only one to emerge, on each occasion, unhurt, smiling" (35). Moleka's danger comes from the fact that his physical passion is not equaled by emotional commitment.

This is not, however, the case with Maru. From the first he is described as the more emotional and soulful one: "It was different with Maru. At the end of a love affair, a deep sorrow would fill his eyes...Maru always fell in love with his women" (35). Maru is also much more patient when it comes to testing his love for Margaret against the racial prejudice in his society. Moleka responds immediately once he falls for Margaret and tries to abolish prejudice on the same day. He deliberately shocks the education supervisor by inviting him to sit down to dinner at table with his Bushmen servants.

Yet in the course of their rivalry for Margaret, it is Maru who tests Moleka's commitment and finds it wanting. As head of the tribal administration, Moleka has provided Margaret with a place to live and furniture. As the future paramount chief and his superior, Maru poses as a tribal traditionalist to test Moleka and demands the return of the bed that he gave Margaret. When he gives in and reclaims the bed, Moleka fails to act on his love for Margaret publicly and defend her against the anti-Bushman prejudice, thus showing himself to be unworthy of her love. His passion is not socially strong enough to confront a greater power than his own. Margaret later acknowledges this limitation of Moleka's by saving, "He will never approach me, because I am a Masarwa" (94).

Maru is content to bide his time and pose as a traditional racialist because he is in control of virtually all the action in the book. He does not pity Margaret's plight and maintains his distance from her on the surface even as he secretly plans to marry her. His love for a Bushwoman is purely idealistic and will lead him to renounce his tribal powers. He does not accept the racism of his people, but will not challenge it directly. Instead, he imagines his love as the basis of a new and different world. He says, "I was not born to rule this mess. If I have a place it is to pull down the old structures and create the new" [68]. His love for Margaret grows as he comes to appreciate her paintings of village scenes. Margaret's art is a compensation for her social isolation and powerlessness. As he collects her paintings through his sister Dikeledi, Maru becomes convinced that Margaret shares with him the imaginative power to create a new world of equality and love. He says, "Look! Don't you see! We are the people who have the strength to build a new world!" [108]. One reason for the idealistic optimism that underlies Maru is the important role given to the powers of imagination that link the artist and the man who loves her because of her gift. Yet Margaret's art is also a power that threatens her because it exceeds her ability to control it: "She could not discipline and control the power machine of production"(101). And it drives her over the edge into two days of total collapse and breakdown. Margaret is not in control of either of the positive forces that shape her life, love or art. Both are potentially destructive and the outcome of the ambivalent tensions that shape Margaret's fate are in doubt until the end of the book: "The events, when they occurred, went off, one after the other like bombs" (115). Satisfied that he will never win Margaret from Maru, Moleka marries Dikeledi and his restless nature subsides. But Margaret reacts as if her neck had been broken. Love fells her and she cannot rise from her bed. Strangely Maru, who has arranged the marriage of his sister and his rival to get Moleka out of the way, reacts to the news of Margaret's serious incapacity with aloofness. "Let her suffer a bit," he says. "It will teach her to appreciate other things"(120). It is the comment of a distant uncaring god rather than a lover and future husband. In fact, Maru does play the role of god in the novel. He drives the evil totems from the village and eventually he also rescues Margaret from the living death he has helped to place her in. But first she must purge herself of her self-pity. "Other people have suffered more than you," he tells her. "You must stop this self-pity"(123). Finally at the end, they leave Dilepe forever, "...heading for a home, a thousand miles away where the sun rose, new and new and new each day"(125). What Maru becomes for Margaret at the end is not so much her lover as the sound of her own abstract hopes: "He was not just anything but some kind of strange, sweet music you could hear over and over again" (124). And the final message of achievement in the book is not so much about the power of personal love as the socially liberating effect that the marriage of Maru and Margaret has on the Bushmen, where "...the wind of freedom had also reached people of the Masarwa tribe"(127).

So *Maru* is a rather strange love story. The sexual side of love that Moleka represents is threatening and destructive. Yet the more positive and soulful love of Maru is very distant. Its power does not directly threaten Margaret, but it is also bound up with power and manipulation—the power of a distant god. In the end it brings about good rather than evil, but it also suggests that suffering is an essential part of life. The fairy tale aspect of love derives from its mysterious power as a force for good that can rescue victims of evil. It comes from men whose power to wield it renders them godlike, and they bestow it upon women who earn it through suffering. This is true not just for Margaret but also for Dikeledi, who is the equal of the men in terms of social class but not in terms of gender. The importance of love ultimately grows as much from its power to produce social change as personal fulfilment. For a heroine like Margaret Cadmore, however, whose character is built on idealism, suffering and art, progressive idealism both provides and substitutes for personal fulfilment.

Most of Bessie Head's work is set in the traditional world of Botswana in which men dominate women. In such a society it is no wonder that a man like Maru who seeks to escape from his own power as a chief and find a better world should be treated like a god and possess the power of one. Though *Maru* ends happily, it contains in the character of Moleka and the threatening effect he has on Margaret, the seeds that will explode into flowers of evil in *A Question of Power*. Unlike *Maru*, in which the men were treated like gods, the male characters who possess absolute power over women and who use it for evil in the later novel will come to be regarded as the devil.

A Question of Power dramatizes the mental breakdown of a character named Elizabeth who is very much like Margaret Cadmore. Another powerless outsider, she is a coloured South African who has come to teach in a Botswana village. The two important male characters, Sello and Dan, also possess enormous power over Elizabeth. This time the forces of evil predominate over the forces of good and the result is madness that includes horribly destructive physical and spiritual incapacity. The battleground shifts from the social world of the Botswana village to the character's inner life and becomes a struggle for Elizabeth's mind and soul. One of the two male characters, Sello, said to be Elizabeth's twin soul, is a Dr. Jekyll and Mr. Hyde character with extreme tendencies toward both good and evil. This moral ambivalence with its premonitions of destruction contributes to Elizabeth's first breakdown and hospitalization. But it is only a prelude to the torment that follows which is inflicted on Elizabeth by the other male figure of complete evil, Dan. The parallels to *Maru* are clearly drawn in his character: he is a friend of Sello's, a cattle millionaire and an African nationalist—a composite of the totems of evil in the previous novel. Not just a traditional African prince, he now becomes a prince of darkness who dominates and tortures Elizabeth through his uncontrolled sexuality. In *Maru* the momentum swung from Moleka's appealing but unfaithful sexuality to Maru's idealistic love. Now in *A Question of Power* the direction is tragically reversed and demonic male sexuality is dominant.

The moral pendulum that finally swung towards good in *Maru* now swings back with a vengeance toward evil in the later novel. Both directions come from the intense isolation of the heroines and their need for men and a dream of love: "...Elizabeth had no experience of love, but she had powerful imaginings about it; its quality and beauty were like a deep, hidden symphony in their heart" [*A Question of Power*, 86]. At first she seems like a more developed version of Margaret Cadmore. She has a little son but no husband. Where Margaret was innocent of love, Elizabeth has an aching need of it which makes her more vulnerable to the torments of sexuality. Once again, male sexuality will be associated with dominant power, fear and finally in the case of Dan, with evil. His sexual drive will be equated with an ambition to rule the world and compared to Hitler and Napoleon. It is a drive for absolute power applied to evil ends.

The other basis of Elizabeth's vulnerability is her own fear that she lacks sexuality. Both Dan and the female figure in her nightmares, Medusa, torment her with the assertion that she does not have a vagina and completely lacks sexuality. Her brief marriage in South Africa to a sex-driven philanderer has left her with negative and fearful imaginings of sex. So Dan's torture of her is inflicted through her dreams of his insatiable sexual activities with an endless parade of women, each one named for her flagrant sexual attributes: Miss Wriggly-Bottom, Miss Sewing Machine, Miss Body Beautiful and the Womb, among others. Initially Elizabeth finds Dan sexually appealing and that, of course, is what makes him so dangerous. His first dream kiss excites her (106). Once again, the most dangerous aspect of sexuality is that it is a force beyond control, just as it was for the women who loved Moleka. As Dan continues his sexual rampages he also assumes the identity of a homosexual and a child molester. In this nightmarish process, out-of-control sexuality leads ultimately to destructive evil. As Elizabeth's madness deepens, she begins to confuse Dan's destructive powers with the previously ambivalent figure of Sello who was at first described as her own twin soul. At one point it is reported that Sello molested his own child and also killed a small boy. Elizabeth's second breakdown begins when she posts a sign in the village post office that states, "Sello is a filthy pervert who sleeps with his daughter" (175). Now Elizabeth herself has a small son whom she largely ignores during her illness and who is cared for by white friends. As rampaging sexuality becomes associated in her mind with perversion and even murder, she seems to transfer her own fears on to Sello who loses whatever positive qualities he once seemed to have. It is this great fear of destructive sexuality that causes Elizabeth to deny her own sexual impulses. At another point she says that if she were a man, she would quickly marry Kenosi, her Botswana woman colleague in the garden where she works. But again, any chance of even admitting a lesbian attraction is immediately dropped.

In *Maru*, it will be remembered, Moleka's sexuality was an attractive but threatening force, rooted in infidelity and destructive to women. But male love was divided as in a fairy tale between the dangerous Moleka and the pure and safe Maru. Both possessed tremendous power over women, but fortunately Maru acted like a god in rescuing the heroine. In *A Question of Power*, however, evil predominates, men also dominate women and uncontrolled sexuality leads to destruction. Perhaps it was because men were held up as gods in *Maru* that Elizabeth must now suffer such hellish evil inflicted by male devils. To apply Zora Neal Hurston's term to Bessie Head's heroines, "Their eyes were watching God," while they were ambushed by a sexual devil. In trying to focus on love as a purely idealistic force, Margaret was able to avoid the dangers of sex. But they certainly caught up to Elizabeth with a vengeance. Perhaps in trying to ignore such natural inclinations completely, Head's characters were left with only an exaggerated and excessive version of sexuality. So Elizabeth, who mostly ignores her young son, is driven mad by the images of Sello and Dan as child molesters. Nightmarish exaggerations of evil in *A Question of Power* balance the fairy tale exaggerations of good in *Maru*. In both the heroines are manipulated supernaturally by gods or devils. And the seeds of one are contained in the other. Elizabeth says of Sello that, "He half showed me that the source of human suffering was God itself, personalities in possession of powers or energies of the soul" [190]. A complementary ambivalence about the moral nature of people connects the two novels.

Like Margaret Cadmore, Elizabeth suffers from the absence of control over her own destiny. Both are passive and innocent; but while Margaret can remain "pure" like the fairy tale heroine Sleeping Beauty, Elizabeth is tormented by the fear of her own evil. Her first breakdown occurs when she begins to scream in a store, "Oh, you bloody bastard Botswana" (51)! His an expression of revenge for her own isolation as an outsider in the village, her weak cry suddenly slipped over into a scream of racial frustration and hatred. This volcanic explosion releases her inner voice that privately insists, "You don't really like Africans" (51). Likewise, both Medusa and Dan develop their power over her by stimulating her own repressed sexual feelings. And in Elizabeth's nightmare good and innocence are powerless to withstand the assault of evil sexuality. She "was never to regain a sense of security or stability on the question of how patterns of goodness were too soft, to indefinable to counter the tumultuous roar of evil" (159).

The common thread that links Elizabeth to Margaret is powerlessness. It is the shared vulnerability of the subjugated racial minority—the Bushman woman and the coloured woman from South Africa in Botswana—as well as the powerlessness of women in a male dominated society where sexual promiscuity is a sign of male power. This last factor is considered by Bessie Head to be the major defect of a traditional African society like Botswana. As she says, "the social defects of Africa are, first, the African man's loose care-free sexuality" (137). This critique of Head's is developed even further in her later collection of short stores, *The Collector of Treasures*.

So the women in Bessie Head's fiction suffer from a double, even a triple sense of powerlessness; as women and as blacks who are also outsiders in a traditional African society. Is it any wonder that they need a fairy tale of saving love to dream about and that they suffer madness as a result of racism, male domination and irresponsible sexuality.

Fortunately, Elizabeth is able to outlast her torture and like Margaret she exhibits the heroic virtue of endurance. At the end of her nightmare Dan finally gives way to Sello who again represents the positive side of man carrying in his travelling bag the message of brotherhood. At the end Head can pull Elizabeth back from her mental torment into her old world of idealism. Once again people as a whole represent the image of God rather than one individual: "There is only one God and his name is man. And Elizabeth is his prophet" (206). Even Head's choice of language retains that underlying ambivalence of gender. But we can now appreciate Elizabeth's suffering as part of her prophetic gift. Like the artist Margaret who suffered to produce her work, Elizabeth is an idealist who suffers alienation and madness for her belief in the goodness of mankind. Lord knows, womankind has long suffered to preserve that dream.

As Elizabeth falls asleep at the end of the novel for what the reader hopes will be her first peaceful night in over a year, "...she placed one soft hand over her land. It was a gesture of belonging" [206]. It is also a moving gesture of healing, in which the divided aspects of her character come together in a final act of self-acceptance and peace; when two finally become one.

As someone who knew Bessie Head in Botswana, I can attest to the fact that her personal struggle was indeed very real, but it never defeated her belief in people. Her work stands as a testament to the hope for a better world, and the drive to write under great adversity was one to which she completely dedicated her life until its end. About this achievement it seems appropriate to remember the words spoken over one of the most enduring of Shakespeare's tragic idealists:

"And flights of angels sing thee to thy rest."

Works Cited

Head, Bessie. *Maru*, (London: Heinemann, 1971).
_____. *A Question of Power*, (London: Heinemann, 1974).

Windows of Womanhood

Ezenwa - Ohaeto

The short stories of Bessie Head encapsulate thematically the richness of her concern with family life and the realities of the South African environment. It is not strange that these short stories crystallize succinct experiences because short stories by their nature convey "the sudden unforgettable revelation of character; the vision of a world through another's eyes; the glimpse of truth; the capture of a moment in time: (Crane, 1). Bessie Head fulfills these requirements because she uses materials that are not only necessary for her short stories but also relevant to the major preoccupation of her writings in justification of the view that "the short story must fly to the very centre of the target" (Grandsaigne and Spackey: 74). Head thus conceives her works as reflecting the process of treading a small, careful pathway through life and she confesses: "All my work is scaled down to this personality need, with the universe itself seen through the eyes of small individual life dramas " ("Biographical Notes", 97). These life dramas enable the author to use her short stories as windows on womanhood and this paper examines these windows through which she explores the various aspects of family life in *The Collector of Treasures*.

The thirteen short stories in this collection are diverse and they portray different aspects of family life. Women feature prominently in these stories but not as isolated characters because it is their relationship with men that animate family life. However this animation is capable of degenerating into negative emotional involvements because human nature is patterned into individual complexities through the possession and mixture of vices and virtues. Bessie Head, however, does not encounter impediments in the creation of human characters because according to Al Imfeld she "is a skillful psychologist. Her work is so full of human magic -- the fathoming of people's minds..." (27). She deepens her stories through this ability to cast insight on the deeper levels of humanity, beneath the physical veneer, into the soul.

Many of the stories in *The Collector of Treasures* could be analysed in pairs as contrastive delineations of family life. The mythological story entitled "The Deep River: A Story of Ancient Tribal Migration" contrasts with the story entitled "Heaven is Not Closed." In the story, "The Deep River," there is a man known as Sebembele who is courageous enough to sacrifice his happiness and kingdom in order to live with the woman Rankwanna, whom he loves. In the traditional society in which this story is set, it is not the moral issues that really fascinate the people but acts that involve brave and firm decisions. On the other hand the woman known as Galethebege in "Heaven is Not Closed" sacrifices her happiness in the church in order to live with the man known as Rolakae, whom she loves. The choices of Sembembele and Galethebege are thus choices that Bessie Head has used to underline the need for creating harmony in family life and that the sacrifices for its success could be performed by either the man or the woman.

Similarly the stories entitled "The Village Saint" and "Jacob: the Story of a Faith-Healing Priest" are contrastive. The "Village Saint" is a story which exposes the hypocrisy of human nature. It also reveals the essence of the aphorism which states that beneath the superficial facade of goodness, deviousness and evil could be concealed. Mma-Mompati succeeds in exploiting the two men in her life: her husband and son. She takes all their wages without leaving anything for them until they break away from her stranglehood. The people then discover that beneath the mask of Mma-Mompati, who carries the Bible and is always preaching, lies a wicked soul. Bessie Head describes the final scene where the son breaks the yoke of exploitation with sarcasm:

> At the end of the next month, Mompati walked straight to his own flat and handed his pay-packet intact to his wife, ate a good supper and fell into a sound sleep after many nights of worry and anguish. The following morning he left for work without even a glance at his mother's home. Then the storm burst. The post of God and Jesus were blown in the winds and the demented vampire behind it was too terrible to behold. She descended on her daughter-in-law with fury (*Collector*, p. 18).

The significance of this story on family life is that Head does not perceive women as possessing all the virtues. She ironically presents the view that womanhood incorporates both virtuous and devilish women. She then implies that harmony of family life lies with reciprocity and not exploitation of either party involved in the relationship.

The story entitled "Jacob: The Story of a Faith-Healing Priest," is used by Bessie Head to contrast the story "The Village Saint." In the story of Jacob the author creates a woman named Johannah (who has been disappointed in love) as a positive influence through which Jacob is reconciled with the warmth of family life. The adversities encountered by Jacob through becoming an orphan at the age of six, his unhappy childhood and subsequent misfortune imposed by poverty are erased by the happiness that he finds in Johannah. Johannah thus contrasts Mma-Mompati in terms of the capacity of women to enrich family life. The entrance of Johannah transforms Jacob who "soon found that his home was run peacefully with clock work precision, by a woman full of the traditions and customs as his upbringing had been that of an outcast living apart from the household and it was as though he was transported back into a childhood he might have had, had his mother lived (*Collector*, p. 34). The story also illustrates the effectiveness of family life on the refinement of the children into disciplined adults. Bessie Head adds a twist to the story by making the greatest rival of Jacob known as Lebojang end his life in disgrace. The two stories show that women must feel a sense of belonging and can only do so by participating fully in the powerful, controlling positions from which the destiny of the society is determined but this desire cannot be achieved in chaos which is why the success of family life becomes important. This window of womanhood which Bessie Head has opened and through which we recognize some female characters caught in moments of intense self-examination illustrate that Bessie Head "is a crusader for sexual and social justice for all men and women. Her favourite theme is the drama of interpersonal relationships and their possibility for individual growth and regeneration" (Ola, 39). However the women could also create problems for themselves amounting in some instances to self-doubt and irrelevant jealousies.

Jealousy and envy thus feature in the short stories entitled "Life" and "Witchcraft" although matters of sex dominate their subject matter. In "Life," Head transfers the conflicts, tension and paradoxes of city life to the village. The relationship between the woman known as Life and the man, Lesego has all the trappings of impending tragedy, for Lesego has the deadly aura of city gangsters. Furthermore the impending doom is inevitable because the creation of an hotel in the village or anywhere for that matter where it could attract humanity is bound to generate terrible deeds. Bessie Head makes persuasive to the reader the consequences of the collision of two worlds: the world of a woman who "has broken all the social taboos" (p. 40) and the world of a man who "had a way of keeping his head above water," (p. 41). The warning Lesego gives to life after their marriage that he would kill her if he sees her with any man is significant in its explanation of his concept of family life. However the maintenance of family life stifles Life who complains once: "I think I have made a mistake. Married life doesn't suit me" (p. 44). It is therefore unsurprising that Life rebels against the regimentation of womanhood involved in family life by committing adultery, which makes Lesego kill her. One of the most significant aspects of this story is the comment by Sianana when he says that "there are good women and good men but they seldom join their lives together. It's always this mess and foolishness ..." (p. 48), which apparently codified Head's view about the reality of family life. The disorganization which such unstable relationships generate in human affairs affect family life and they lead to tragedies.

Contrastively, in the short story entitled "Witchcraft," the woman known as Mma-Mabele is unwilling to give herself to men, unlike Life who is willing. Although Head writes that "the only value women were given in the society was their ability to have sex; there was nothing beyond that," (p. 49), the story reflects the latent indomitable will of responsible women. Mma-Mabele survives because as she confesses to people: "I cannot sit down because I am too poor and there is no one else to feed my children" (p. 56). The resilience exhibited by this woman is therefore used to portray that survival depends more on individual will than recourse to extraneous solutions. Mma-Mabele indicates the fulfilling essence of womanhood which is hinged on the ability of women to contribute positively to the progress of family life.

Bessie Head is obviously interested in presenting two dimensions to womanhood in these short stories because her protagonists consist of women who are capable of creating and women who are capable of destroying. In the story, "Looking for a Rain God" the sacrifice of the two little girls which is performed in order to induce rain in the time of drought is unfulfilled and it epitomizes the fact that in times of extreme adversity humanity is placed on the precarious edge of insanity. The drought is thus one of the symbols through which Head casts insight on family life. The two little girls are part of the family but in the bid to save themselves the Mokgobija family with the support of its women commit a heinous crime illustrating the absurdity implied in the destruction of children in order to save adults. Although the men are the tools for this wanton destruction, they are goaded by the ritual chant of the women who are desperate for rain.

The stories are as varied as they are peopled with diverse characters. In the story "Kgotla" the marital difficulties caused by the blind man Gobosamang are used to present another aspect of womanhood in contradiction to the behaviour of the Mokgobija women who contributed in destroying their children. The behaviour of Rose, the beautiful woman married to the blind Gobosamang is a metaphor for stressing not only the intrinsic virtue of some woman to sacrifice their lives in order to make family life a success but also the consequences of envy and jealousy. Most members of the community cannot understand how a beautiful woman can tie herself to an incapacitated man and the author apparently portrays that envy is a handicap to family life.

More diverse characters are also involved in the story "The Wind and the Boy" which traces the special relationship between the illegitimate Friedman and his grandmother Mma-Sejosenye, which also intensifies the emotional involvements in family life. The reaction of Mma-Sejosenye to the untimely death of Friedman illustrates this deep seated emotional involvement which makes womanhood an invaluable aspect in the construction of family relationships. Women are by nature closer to the children. Children regard women as protectors and guides. Hence, women who do not have clear ideas regarding the development of children often contribute to the confusion children experience in their relationships to society. Mma-Sejosenye is aware of these societal requirements because she is involved in family life to the extent that the shock of Friedman's death kills her. Furthermore this story also reveals the encroachment of unbridled modernism on the sleepy villages and its attendant devastations. But within these societal pressures Bessie Head shows women who are part of and at the same time apart from the politics of personal lives because they make decisions that affect their neighbours and they are apart because within each individual is the will to submit or oppress other people. Moreover, it has been observed that Head "does not create characters who are at all interested in the official, political sphere but they are concerned about their local communities, their families, their neighbours and themselves" (Geurts: 48). This personal politics is a substratum of the general politics of the society which makes progressive women an essential requirement for the development of womanhood and society.

Modernism in family life is reflected in the stories "Snapshots for a Wedding" and "The Special One". In "Snapshots for a wedding", Kegoletile has a choice between taking either Neo or Mathata as a wife but the women do not possess such opportunities. The relevance of this story to womanhood is that the society fashions normative chains that bind women and these chains are what Bessie Head feels are debilitating and detrimental to the happiness of family life. The thematic importance of this story to the problems of womanhood and family life becomes graphic in the other complementary story "The Special One." The story is complementary in the sense that it proceeds further to reveal the anatomy of family life through Gaenametse who is regarded as a woman with an unstable mind because she desires emotional satisfaction from the husband. The message in this story is that women have all the emotional feelings generated by family life and that their satisfaction depends on the abilities of their partners to be sensitive to their basic emotional requirements. The women featured in this story are thus used to indicate the impossibility of shrouding positive emotions and the consequences of obliterating self-satisfaction. Furthermore Head apparently uses this story to make telling commentaries on human relationships because the story is suffused with statements condemning the marginalization of women. One of the characters known as Mrs. Maleboge laments: "I lost ... because women are just dogs in this society" (p. 81). The author confirms her support of this view through the comment of the narrator who states that, "the old days of polygamy are gone and done with, but the men haven't yet accepted that the women want them to be monogamists" (p. 86). The behaviour of Gaenametse thus portrays the need for women to be regarded as human beings who also require emotional fulfilment. It is on this basis that the story "The Special One" becomes symbolic of the motivations and subtle forces necessary in building good family life which coalesce into the invaluable need for mutual understanding.

The title story, "The Collector of Treasures," examines in greater details this need for understanding for womanhood in family life, through the women jailed for killing their husbands. The reasons for the actions of the women range from Kebonye's complaint that "our men do not think that we need tenderness and care," (p. 89) to the narrator's description that "there were really only two kinds of men in the society. The one kind created such misery and chaos that he could be broadly damned as evil ... since that kind of man was on the majority in the society he needed a little analysing as he was responsible for the complete breakdown of family life" (p. 91). This image of the male destroyer of family life is perceived by the author as prevalent and his faults are magnified by the rewards of independence which generated more wealth for both the faithful dedicated worker and the libertine. Contrastively Bessie Head is not blind to the fact that human beings possess both negative and positive aspects because the narrator reveals that "there was another kind of man in the society with the power to create himself anew. He turned all his resources, both emotional and material, towards his family life ..." (p. 93). The reaction of Dikeledi in killing her husband, Garesego, who deserted her and the children but who comes back to her house one day in order to satisfy his ego is symptomatic of the inconsideration that could cause tragedies in family life. Garesego epitomizes all the vices of those men who could be damned as evil due to the chaos and misery they generate and he is quite unlike Paul Thebolo, the oasis of goodness, who promises to take care of the children of Dikeledi when she goes to jail. Moreover the four women who serve as companions to Dikeledi in jail have killed their husbands. The author is obviously using the story of these women (two of them killed their husbands by cutting off their genital organs) to illustrate the injustices that insensitive people could inflict on the psyche and mental equilibrium of their partners in family life. The story also indicates the violence that could erupt if most of the oppressive societal sanctions on womanhood are left unchallenged as sacrosanct. It is thus right to point out the observation which states that "the sexual politics dictated by traditional patriarchy and the double standards which are upheld with equanimity, oppress Head's women and lead them to seek desperate and violent methods of changing those inherent inequalities. Head focuses on certain types of strong women who attempt to redefine their lives, who break acceptable social codes or behaviour, become outcasts, and who are ultimately destroyed for this act of controlling their personal/biological selves" (Katrak, 32). These women who strive to change the system through acts of personal courage are not really destroyed for in their refusal to subsume their individuality to the society's definitions of family roles lies an inspirational symbol for other women.

It is significant that Bessie Head ends her collection of short stories with the story of Tholo and Thato in the story entitled "Hunting." This story reveals another angle to family life through the understanding and generosity of the couple. Moreover this story negates the narrator's comment that "men were not particularly interested in the women and they certainly did not value them. They never gave a thought to the damage they were inflicting on the women -- women became hard and callous with no values or tenderness or respect to cling to" (p. 106). This story thus shows that when there is tenderness and respect in family life that it is possible for the couple to live like Tholo and Thato in the creation of good family life. This story is thus parobolic for it indicates that women respond with warmth and love when they are confronted with those same emotions and attitudes.

Bessie Head therefore reveals in the short stories in *The Collector of Treasures* that humanity has diverse threads which could be woven into a fine cloth of family life depending on the manner in which womanhood is moulded to fit into an appropriate loom. She does not blame men excessively because she is aware that womanhood imposes its own unpleasant limitations to a happy family life. She is, however, interested in the fulfillment of the individual because some of the stories contain instances of women producing illegitimate children but these unwanted pregnancies are not used to either ridicule the women or make their lives a misery. It is then clear that Head does not believe that womanhood should be regimented by the hypocritical eyes of the society.

The short stories are essentially conceived from the moral angle especially in terms of the issues of family life. Bessie Head shows that she believes in the dictum which states that mistakes always occur and that any individual who slips in life must not be turned into an object of derision. These stories are thus symbolic because in each of them "a woman plays a leading role and provides the focus from which all other characters are considered and evaluated. Many of the stories are used to make social and political comments, especially as they relate to the status of women in modern African society -- the village under focus is used as a microcosm of traditional Africa at large" (Taiwo, 198). The stories thus function as windows through which womanhood has been examined in order to cast insight on family life. Bessie Head has therefore used her short stories to display imaginative skill in stressing that both male and female characters could possess noteworthy virtues despite the abhorrent vices of their kind. She has through *The Collector of Treasures* codified stories that could be used to understand humanity better in order to make family life a success.

Works Cited

Crane, Milton ed. "What Makes a Great Short Story?", *Great Short Stories* (New York: Bantam Books, 1971 edition).

Geurts, Kathryn. "Personal Politics in the Novels of Bessie Head", *Presence Africaine* No. 140 (4th Quarterly 1986), 47-74.

Grandsaigne, Jean de and Gary Spackey "The African Short Story Written in English: A Survey", *Ariel* Vol. 15, No. 2 (April 1984), 73-85.

Head, Bessie, "Biographical Notes: A Seearch for Historical COntinuity and Roots", in Ernest Emenyonu ed. *Literature and Society: Selected Essays on African Literature* (Oguta, Nigeria: Zim-Pan Publishers, 1986), 95-103.

_____, *The Collector of Treasures* (London: Heinemann, 1977).

Imfeld, Al. "Bessie Head" in Dieter Brauer and Rudolf Strobinger. eds. *African Writers on the Air* (Dw-Dokumente, 3. Cologne: Deutsche Welle, 1984), 26-33.

Katrak, Ketu H. "From Pauline to Dikeledi: The Philosophical and Political Vision of Bessie Head's Protagonists", *Ba Shiru* Vol. 12, No. 2 (1985), 26-35.

Ola, Virginia. "Women's Role in Bessie Head's Ideal World", *Ariel* Vol. 17, No. 4 (October 1986), 39-47.

Taiwo, Oladele "Bessie Head," *Female Novelists of Africa* (London: Macmillan Publishers, 1984), 1985-214.

Contributors

Cecil A. Abrahams is Professor English and Dean of the Faculty of Humanities at Brock University. The author of books on William Blake and Alex La Guma, he has published widely in journals throughout the world.

Bessie Head was born in South Africa but lived much of her adult life in Botswana. Through her novels, stories, essays and histories, she has brought Botswana history to life.

Carol Davison completed her Master of Arts degree at York University in Canada and is doing doctoral work on Commonwealth Literature.

Roger Berger teaches at Grand Valley State University.

Nancy Topping Bazin is a Professor of English at Old Dominion University in Virginia.

Ella Robinson is a Professor of English at the University of Nebraska in Lincoln.

Virginia Ola is Head of the Department of English at the University of Benin in Nigeria.

Femi Ojo-Ade, a Nigerian, was until recently Visiting Professor at Spelman College in Atlanta, Georgia.

Nigel Thomas teaches literature at the Université Laval in Canada.

Ezenwa-Ohaeto is a Lecturer in the English Department of Anambra State College of Education in Nigeria.

Daniel Gover teaches at Keane College in New Jersey.

Horace Goddard teaches at Concordia University in Canada.

Best Selections/AWP Series of Books

OPERATION TIMBER: Pages From the Savimbi Dossier
edited with an introduction by William Minter
ISBN: 0-86543-103-5   Cloth $19.95
          0-86543-104-3   Paper $ 6.95

AFROCENTRICITY *by Molefi Kete Asante*
ISBN: 0-86543-067-5   Paper $9.95

PROPHETIC FRAGMENTS *by Cornel West*
ISBN: 0-86543-085-3   Cloth $17.95

**THE TIES THAT BIND:African-American Consciousness of
Africa** *by Bernard Magubane*
ISBN: 0-86543-036-5   Cloth $32.00
          0-86543-037-3   Paper $ 9.95

WHITHER SOUTH AFRICA? *edited by Bernard Magubane
& Ibbo Mandaza*
ISBN: 0-86543-048-9   Cloth $29.95
          0-86543-049-7   Paper $ 9.95

**FRANCOPHONE AFRICAN FICTION: Reading a Literary
Tradition** *by Jonathan Ngate*
ISBN: 0-86543-087-X   Cloth $32.00
          0-86543-088-8   Paper $ 9.95

**FULCRUMS OF CHANGE: Origins of Racism in the Americas
and other essays** *by Jan Carew*
ISBN: 0-86543-032-2   Cloth $29.95
          0-86543-033-0   Paper $ 9.95

**CONSCIENCE ON TRIAL/WHY I WAS DETAINED: Notes
of a Political Prisoner in Kenya** *by Koigi wa Wamwere*
ISBN: 0-86543-063-2   Cloth $25.95
          0-86543-064-0   Paper $8.95

ENDGAME IN SOUTH AFRICA? *by Robin Cohen*
ISBN: 0-86543-090-X   Cloth $24.95
          0-86543-091-8   Paper $ 7.95

DUMBA NENGUE: RUN FOR YOUR LIFE/Peasant Tales of Tragedy in Mozambique by *Lina Magaia*
ISBN: 0-86543-073-X   Cloth $14.95
        0-86543-074-8   Paper $ 6.95

UNDER A SOPRANO SKY by *Sonia Sanchez*
ISBN: 0-86543-052-7   Cloth $16.95
        0-86543-053-5   Paper $ 6.95

AID & DEVELOPMENT IN SOUTHERN AFRICA: Evaluating a Participatory Learning Process *edited by Denny Kalyalya, Khethiwe Mhlanga, Ann Seidman, Joseph Semboja*
ISBN: 0-86543-046-2   Cloth $25.95
        0-86543-047-0   Paper $7.95

BLACK AFRICA: The Economic and Cultural Basis for a Federated State by *Cheikh Anta Diop*
ISBN: 0-86543-058-6   Paper $7.95

PRECOLONIAL BLACK AFRICA by *Cheikh Anta Diop*
ISBN: 0-86543-070-5   Paper $8.95

MARCUS GARVEY: Anti-Colonial Champion by *Rupert Lewis*
ISBN: 0-86543-061-6   Cloth $29.95
        0-86543-062-4   Paper $11.95

THE COLONIAL LEGACY IN CARIBBEAN LITERATURE by *Amon Saba Saakana*
ISBN: 0-86543-059-4   Cloth $24.95
        0-86543-060-8   Paper $ 7.95

WOMEN IN AFRICAN LITERATURE TODAY edited by *Eldred Durosimi Jones, Eustace Palmer, Marjorie Jones*
ISBN: 0-86543-056-X   Cloth $29.95
        0-86543-057-8   Paper $ 8.95

IF THIS IS TREASON, I AM GUILTY by *Allan A. Boesak*
ISBN: 0-86543-055-1   Paper $7.95

ON TRANSFORMING AFRICA: Discourse with Africa's Leaders by *Kofi Buenor Hadjor*
ISBN: 0-86543-044-6   Cloth $25.95
        0-86543-045-4   Paper $ 7.95

RASTA AND RESISTANCE by *Horace Campbell*
ISBN: 0-86543-034-9   Cloth $32.95
        0-86543-035-7   Paper $10.95